Comedian, writer and broadcast[...] co-host of Triple J's Breakfast sh[...] national brekkie radio gigs, and f[...] 'The Glass House'.

However, he is probably still best known as one of Australia's greatest live stand-up comedians, selling out theatres across the country. His ease on stage is a disarming front for intelligent material that ranges from personal to pop to politics. He has also performed at the Melbourne Comedy Festival and the Adelaide Fringe Festival, and in 1999 was nominated for the Perrier Best Newcomer Award at the Edinburgh Fringe Festival, returning since to much critical acclaim.

Wil writes the 'Sunday Roast' column for the *Sunday Magazine* (*Sunday Telegraph* and *Herald-Sun*). He has also been a columnist for *The Australian*, *Melbourne Extra* (1998-99) and *The Big Issue* (1997), and is one of Australia's most accomplished corporate performers. He currently hosts the successful Wil & Lehmo show on Triple M.

SURVIVAL OF THE DUMBEST

WIL ANDERSON

RANDOM HOUSE AUSTRALIA

Survival of the Dumbest is based on a selection of Wil Anderson's 'Sunday Roast' columns in the *Sunday Magazine*, which appears in the *Sunday Telegraph* and the *Sunday Herald-Sun*.

Random House Australia and the author acknowledge the support of the *Sunday Magazine* in the publication of this book.

Random House Australia Pty Ltd
Level 3, 100 Pacific Highway, North Sydney, NSW 2060
www.randomhouse.com.au

Sydney   New York   Toronto
London   Auckland   Johannesburg

First published by Random House Australia 2006. This edition published 2007.

Copyright © Wil Anderson 2006.

National Library of Australia
Cataloguing-in-Publication Entry

Anderson, Wil, 1974–.
Survival of the dumbest.

ISBN 978 1 74166 747 9 (pbk.).

1. Australian wit and humour. 2. Humorous stories,
Australian. 3. Stupidity – Australia – Anecdotes. I.
Title.

A827.4

Cover and internal photograph by James Penlidis
Cover design by Greendot Design
Internal design by Greendot Design
Typeset in Bembo by Midland Typesetters, Australia
Printed and bound by Griffin Press, South Australia

10 9 8 7 6 5 4 3 2 1

For Amy
The smartest thing I have ever done.

CONTENTS

Only two things are infinite, the universe and human stupidity, and I'm not sure about the former.   Albert Einstein

ACKNOWLEDGEMENTS

G'day folks,

Most of the words in this book first appeared in my 'Sunday Roast' column in the *Sunday Magazine* in the *Sunday Telegraph* and *Sunday Herald-Sun*. (Wow, that's a whole lot of Sundays.)

So first and foremost I'd like to thank Jodi Scott for giving me a blank page and a hell of a lot of creative freedom, and more importantly for answering all the complaint letters from nannas who didn't like my toilet humour and wanted to know what a 'Shannon Noll' was.

Also, a massive shout-out to my long-suffering editor Jo Hawkins who knows that I'm truly at my most creative when trying to think up excuses for why my copy isn't in on time . . . yet again.

Thanks to Jane Palfreyman at Random House who gave me the opportunity to turn the columns into a book, and to Nadine Davidoff who actually did all the hard work. Seriously folks, I just provided the ingredients, she is the real chef here.

A massive thanks must also go to my amazing management team at Token, and all the guys behind the scenes at *The Glass House* and Triple J who rearranged their schedules, and lives, on those days when 'I really had to finish my column'.

To my family, firstly Mum and Dad for being amazingly supportive when their son told them he wanted to throw away a perfectly respectable career and tell dick jokes for cash, and more importantly for not suing for the things I've said, and often exaggerated, about them in this book.

And, of course, to Amy, Tip and Diego, you guys are my life. Thank you for forgiving me all the afternoons and evenings where you wanted to do something fun but I had to write some more knob jokes about Warnie.

On that note, thanks must also go to Shane, Russell, Heath, Shannon, Eddie, John, Mark and Kim, for all those weeks when I had nothing, and you did something. I really couldn't have done this without you.

And, finally, to you guys. Thanks for watching, listening and reading my stuff over the years. You have given me a life that a farm boy from Heyfield never could have dared dream of.

I hope that in return along the way you've have a few laughs. After all, that's why I do it . . . well that, and I have no other skills and a hideous mortgage.

Cheers,
Wil. x

ONE

SURVIVAL OF THE DUMBEST

Sometimes I think we have stopped evolving as a human race. If you need evidence simply read the instructions on the back of almost anything you buy.

I purchased a packet of peanuts the other day, and just reading the labelling made me despair for humanity.

First it was the big bold letters that said: 'Warning, may contain traces of nuts' – well duh – but it was the second line that really pushed me over the edge.

It simply read: 'Instructions, open packet, eat nuts'. Phew, lucky they put that there, I was going to stick them up my butt and then ask someone to pull my finger and do my impression of a poker machine paying out.

But it's not just nuts that have gone nuts. I bought a glass biscuit jar the other day, and it came with instructions. Think about that.

Instructions. I'm sorry, but if you need instructions to open a jar, I don't think you should be trusted with glass.

Is there truly anyone who looks at a jar with a lid on it and thinks: 'But how do I get the bikkies in there? It must be some kind of combination, or magic trick. Damn, I wish this thing had instructions.'

Maybe the people who need that kind of help are also those who buy the deodorant I use. The one that has the warning on the back in big letters that says: 'Do not spray in eyes!'

❖ ❖ ❖

Okay, here's my first question . . . who has sweaty eyes? What moron gets up in the morning and thinks: 'Gee my eyes stink . . . ow, ow, ow there should be a warning!'

I don't mean to sound harsh, but if you need that warning, you're too stupid to read it. (Especially if you have previously sprayed deodorant in your eyes.)

You think that warning is stupid? I got some sleeping pills for an overseas flight once, and on the packet it said: 'Warning, may cause drowsiness!'

Really? Well I'd better have a couple of cups of coffee and some Red Bull to take the edge off then.

That's like having a packet of Aspirin that reads: 'Warning, may relieve the symptoms of a headache' or a packet of Viagra that says 'Warning, may cause Grandpa to chase Grandma around the kitchen table.'

There is actually an electric power drill that comes with the warning: 'Not to be used as a dental drill!'

Yes, it's time for *RPA* meets *Better Homes And Gardens*: 'Look, we have used the drill for the pergola, now let's use it for that troublesome molar.' I'm sorry, but if you need that information on your power-tool, then you are a power-tool.

Or the hair-colouring that comes with the instruction: 'Do not use as an ice-cream topping.' Although to be honest, if you are stoned enough to think that is a good idea, you are probably stoned enough to eat it too. Maybe you are happy to eat in a restaurant where there is hair in the food, you just draw the line at it being grey ones.

Of course, if this really happens, then maybe the opposite is true too. That would explain Ray Martin's hair. Maybe it's just Chocolate Ice-Magic.

Then there was the Pepper Spray that apparently comes with the disclaimer: 'Caution, never aim spray at your own eyes.' Now I have to admit, this does sound like sensible advice. Although I also think if you did spray it in your own eyes, it would warn off your attacker, because they would think you were completely nuts. (And if they did still attack you, at least you wouldn't see them coming.)

Hair-dryers now come with the warning: 'Do not use while taking a shower!' Again I feel like this one falls under heading of moron – at the very least because using it while in the shower must limit its effectiveness. 'I have it on high, but for some reason my hair is still wet!'

This is right up there with the toilet brush that comes with the warning sticker: 'Do not use orally!'

Okay, first, unless you have teeth the size of Larry Emdur, who thinks a toilet brush is a good idea for dental hygiene? I don't care if your toothpaste has whitening, tartar control, baking soda, peroxide and bleach in it – that is still not okay. And second, I have heard of teeth smelling like crap, but come on. What's next, using the toilet duck to gargle?

And let's not forget the cigarette lighter that comes with the advice: 'Do not use near open flame.' You see, I would have thought that would be a much better warning to have on Michael Jackson's face.

I don't have an iPod Shuffle, but according to friends who do, they come with the warning that you shouldn't eat them.

Why would anyone eat their iPod? Do you listen to it, and then think, well I know it makes my ears feel good, I wonder how it would make my tongue feel?

Maybe people just see the band names Cake, Ice-Cream Hands, Reel Big Fish and Bread . . . and just can't resist.

One of my favourites was the dishwasher that came with the instruction: 'Don't allow children to play in the dishwasher.' Although, I guess as long as you provided them with some snorkels it would be a pretty quick way to get them clean. But please, whatever you do, don't dry them off in the oven. Use the microwave, it's much quicker.

Speaking of the kiddies, I also hear that Fruit Roll-ups come with the instruction to 'remove plastic before eating'. Although personally I'm not sure I could tell the difference. I don't even buy Roll-ups anymore – I just get a piece of Glad Wrap and colour it in with texta. (Again, if you need this warning you probably also need one on a Kinder Surprise reminding people not to eat the toy.)

And apparently there is a quite popular brand of Baby Oil that has a warning that says: 'Keep away from children.' Yes, you wouldn't want to use the Baby Oil on babies. It's only for fully grown men who dress in nappies and like to coat themselves in the stuff and be spanked.

Maybe they're hiding something more sinister. I mean, they make macadamia oil out of macadamias, and they make hazelnut oil out of hazelnuts . . . all I am saying is do the maths. Maybe they just get a bunch of infants down the factory and fire up the blender.

(Or p'raps the problem is that they are worried if George W. finds out the babies have oil, the new Axis of Evil will be Iran, North Korea and Kindergarten.)

But without doubt, my absolute, absolute favourite was the mattress that came with the warning: 'Do not attempt to swallow.'

(There is no truth to the rumour that this is what Matt Shirvington has written on the front of his running shorts.)

Now this warning disturbs and amuses me for a couple of reasons. First, it is so random that you know the only reason it is there is because someone has tried. Secondly, how stoned do you have to be before you try and eat a mattress?

I mean, there are not enough marijuana-filled boogie-board

bags in the world to make me try and eat a mattress. How dry would it be? Well, I guess unless you washed it down with a waterbed, and maybe a little hair-dye on top for flavour.

Idiocy is all around us – you just have to open your Lynx-scented eyes. I'll give you another example. I was waiting for a bus the other day, and I noticed on the driver's window there is a little sign that says: 'Do not access bus through window!'

Who is that sign for? Keanu Reeves? People who were born by caesarean and so never go through doors, only through the window? Do they have one on the roof that says: 'Do not access bus by sky-diving'?

Ladies and gentlemen, the simple truth is that there are a lot of simple people in the world.

If you need any further proof, check this out. I read once that in the last ten years, 31 Australians have died from watering the Christmas tree while the lights were still plugged in. What's worse, at least a couple of those were watering plastic trees.

Now I don't want to seem callous, but to me that's not a tragedy – that's natural selection.

You see, from what I can vaguely recall from science at school when we weren't sitting up the back trying to work out how to turn various household items into a bong, there was this bloke called Charles Darwin who came up with the theory of evolution. (And to reward him they named the least evolved city in Australia in his honour.)

In basic terms, it was a matter of Survival of the Fittest. In every generation the strongest and the most intelligent would survive, they would breed together and we would evolve. Well, no more. We have stopped evolving as a human race.

Don't believe me? We live in a time where George W. Bush is the leader of the free world. This is a man Forrest Gump would have hung shit on at school. A man who once said: 'The question is rarely asked, is our children learning?' Most presidents travel on Air Force One, he has to travel on a special bus where they let him lick the windows.

It's no longer Survival of the Fittest, it's Survival of the Dumbest.

And why have we stopped evolving? Well it's simple, all these warnings are keeping the morons alive. And today I have three words for you ladies and gentlemen: Let . . . them . . . go.

I'm serious, if you honestly have a friend who buys a brand new pair of sneakers, gets them home, unpacks them, gets that little package of chemicals out of them and wants to eat them . . . you let them.

It's one less moron to be pissing in the shallow end of our gene pool and we can get back to evolving.

Signs and labelling pander to the already dumb, but there are whole industries that depend on drawing out the dumbarse in all of us. Like product development and advertising.

For example, can we just skip to a razor that has a hundred blades and be done with it? I mention this because I noticed the other day one of the major shaving companies is about to launch a new razor with five blades.

That's right, five blades. Apparently the first one picks up the hair, the second cuts it, the third goes out and picks up your dry-cleaning, the fourth goes to market and the fifth goes 'wee wee wee all the way home'.

So the question has to be asked, just how many blades does one man need? If they keep going at this rate, pretty soon I'll have a blade for every single hair on my face.

Put it this way, you know you're in trouble when even Edward Scissorhands thinks you should slow down. I mean, come on, even Wesley Snipes stopped at three Blades.

(Yes, two movie jokes in a row, this column will be killing the all-important video-store clerk demographic.)

But seriously folks, why could we possibly need five different blades on a razor?

Are razors like boy-bands now? You have to have the blade that can sing, the blade that can dance, the ugly blade, the nerdy blade and the gay blade.

I'm all for progress, but it seems to me any more than one blade is a little unnecessary.

I mean unless the other blades are plucking your eyebrows, trimming your nose and ear hair, and manicuring your bikini line – it seems that one could do the job just fine.

I think it's sad when there are more blades on my razor than in my entire kitchen. These days I'm better off preparing dinner in the bathroom.

It's a vicious cycle. One company adds a blade, so the other adds an extra blade, so then the first company has to add another blade, and that's pretty much how the Cold War started.

What's next, the Gillette Tomahawk, with fifty blades and extra uranium to make sure your hair never grows back?

Maybe Kim Jong Il isn't interested in pursuing a nuclear arms race, maybe he's just interested in keeping his mad dictator's face as smooth as a baby's bottom.

And while I am having my razor rant, who is naming these things? You have The Mach, The Fusion, The Champion, The Turbo, and The Quatro.

It sounds less like the names of razor blades and more like a casting call for a new series of Gladiators.

At the moment I'm using a Mach Turbo, which sounds like something Mark Webber should be driving in the Formula One Grand Prix.

And now I see you can get razors with batteries, that vibrate, and even have something called a 'lubra-strip'.

Let's face it, if they can come up with a razor that gives a good foot massage and plays James Blunt, pretty soon women won't need men at all.

And have you ever read the packaging on these things? My current razor is a Gillette which, according to the blurb, is 'the best a man can get'.

Really? Personally I would have thought any sentence that talked about the 'best a man can get' would have also included the words 'Scarlett Johansson' and 'lap-dance'.

Who wrote that slogan, Dr Seuss? 'Gillette, it's the best a man can get, and if you use it on your pet, you should take them to the vet.'

But I digress. The one thing that shocked me most of all when I read the back of my razor packet is that my razor has its own website. Yes, that's right, I'll repeat that again, my razor has its own website.

I guess that's not the site most people are expecting when they type 'hot' and 'shaved' into Google.

(They will be even more shocked when they type in 'big jugs' and end up at www.tupperware.com.)

But think about this for a moment. With all the infinite possibilities offered by the internet, how bored would you have to be to look up the website for a razor blade?

So anyway, I looked it up.

And check this out, not only does my razor have a website, but it also has its own fan-club. I am not making this up.

Now, I'm sorry, but if you are the sort of person who joins a fan-club for a razor blade then you have a lot more serious problems than a little bum-fluff.

In fact if you are the sort of person who would join a fan-site for a razor, I'm not sure I want you handling a blade.

I'm not sure you should be trusted with anything that close to your face that isn't made of ice-cream.

I don't know about you, but sometimes it really scares me that we live in a world where nobody could name the most recent winner of the Nobel Prize for Physics, but a razor blade has its own fan-club.

I think I'm just going to give up and grow a beard.

TWO
THE DUMB AND THE RESTLESS

I was raised on a farm in rural Victoria just outside a small country town called Heyfield, population 2000. For those who don't know, Heyfield is actually an Aboriginal word that means 'place of limited job opportunities'.

My parents, Chris and Graeme, are dairy farmers, and I spent the first seventeen years of my life in a small house on Anderson's Road, which was actually named after my grandfather who built the road. Yes, cue banjo music now.

But this is nothing compared to my dad, who has spent the past sixty years on the same road. People often ask if my parents are proud of my success. I think they're just proud I'm not married to my sister. (We dated, but it didn't work out.)

Truth be told, I actually loved growing up on the farm, apart from two days a year – Christmas and my birthday. This is when it sucked to be a farm kid because while our friends were getting bikes and toys, we would invariably receive pets as presents.

Now, I don't want to seem ungrateful. I love animals, and I am sure there are plenty of city kids who would love to get a pet as a pressie, but if you grow up on a farm, pets are the worst gift you can get.

Because, let's face it, pets are everywhere on a farm. A farm is nothing but pets; you can choose a cow, sheep or a chicken. To piss off our parents, we would name our pets after what we really wanted for Christmas. We had a cat called Cricket Bat, a dog called Barbie Dream House and a couple of goldfish called Decent Bloody Parents.

But by far the worst thing about farm life was getting up at the crack of dawn to milk the cows. To this day I don't understand why we had to milk the cows at five a.m. Why couldn't we do it at a more civilised hour, like ten? I mean, the cows have bugger-all else to do.

In all my years of milking, I never once saw a cow tapping its watch and saying: 'Hurry up, I've got things to do today! I've got pilates with the horses at seven, I'm helping the chicken across the road at nine, at ten I have to vote with the donkey, and I've got to be home by five to be a steak and a leather jacket by dinner.'

Farm life would have been so much easier if cows were as lazy as humans. I would have loved to overhear my dad get that Monday morning phone call: 'Yeah, g'day Graeme, it's Daisy, mate! Don't think I'll be coming in today. I had a huge weekend on the grass, and now all my four stomachs are playing up. I drank so much, one of my teats is leaking kahlua and milk, and I might even be coming down with a little bit of mad cows'. I think I might have to stay at home and milk myself!'

I still remember the day I told Dad I wasn't interested in becoming a farmer because I didn't want to spend the rest of my life getting up at five o'clock in the morning.

And I still remember what he said when he called me at 3.45 a.m. all those years later on my first day hosting the morning show on Triple J: 'Good luck today son, I'm proud of you. Now I'm just going to sleep in for another hour!'

Let me say that my dad Graeme is a great bloke and he gave me a lot of really good advice when I was growing up, such as: 'Find a job you love, and you will always be happy'; 'Don't eat the yellow snow'; and 'Never make out with a woman who has an Adam's Apple.'

But not everything he said was suitable for a desk calendar. Sometimes he was less Confucius, and more Confuse-Us. For example, I don't think there was ever a more inaccurate phrase than: 'Listen up, son, 'cos I'm only going to say this once ...'

Really, Dad? I think not. In fact, what I'm guessing is you are going to say the same thing over and over and over until I start to suspect there is an echo in our lounge room that's saying: 'Take ... out ... the ... garbage.'

'Don't talk with your mouth full' was another one of his favourites, although I have to agree with this one. After all, if everyone followed this rule, Meatloaf concerts would be a lot shorter, Amanda Vanstone would say a lot less in parliament, and we wouldn't hear from Paris Hilton at all.

One adage I was not so sure of was, 'Good things come in small packages'. I've always suspected it was invented by the same men who came up with, 'Size doesn't matter'; 'It's just cold in here'; and, 'This has never happened before, I swear.'

(Put it this way, if you really want to test the stupidity of this expression, observe your female friends when they watch Matt Shirvington run.)

Another of Graeme's classics was, 'Nobody ever died of hard work!' Well, maybe not, Dad, but hard work has been linked to fatigue, aching feet and blisters, and frankly I'm not willing to risk it. Anyway, if you think about it, the saying isn't even true. In fact, it couldn't be more filled with crap if it participated in a crap-filling competition in Crap Town.

If nobody ever died of hard work, then what happened to the slaves who built the pyramids? What did they die of? Bird flu? Even in modern times, the major causes of death are heart attack and stroke which are often linked to working too hard. You rarely read a newspaper report of someone sustaining a serious, life-threatening X-Box injury . . . or dropping dead after lying on the couch watching *Buffy*.

Of course, at the time I never made any of these points to Dad because I knew that if I'd dared, he would've responded with his trump card: 'Well, nobody likes a smarty pants!' (Silly me for assuming that Dr Karl never made it onto *Cleo*'s Most Eligible Batchelor List because of his shirts. Of course, it does explain why Shane Warne and David Beckham are so popular with the ladies.)

If I really tried to slide a fast one past Dad, he would always bring out the tried and true: 'Do I look like I was born yesterday?' Well no, Dad, you don't, but have you checked out Grandad lately? He is bald, wrinkly, can only eat mashed food and keeps wetting his pants.'

As well as dispensing words of wisdom, my dad had a saying for nearly every situation. 'Laughter is the best medicine' he once told me. But I still can't think of an instance where this might be true. Personally, if I were hit by a bus, I'd rather be treated by Jim the Doctor than Con the Fruiterer. And when I'm in pain, I want a prescription – and not one that reads: 'Take two episodes of *The Simpsons* daily, and if pain persists, please stop watching *Comedy Inc*.'

Let's face it, if laughter truly was the best medicine, paramedics would drive clown cars; you'd be able to claim Billy Connolly tickets on Medicare; and emergency wards would ring with cries of, 'Hey Nurse, get me some nitrous oxide, a Christmas bon-bon, and last Saturday's *Funniest Home Videos* stat!'

(Not that the nurses would have time to work. They'd be too busy running away from bald men to the Benny Hill theme.)

Here's another one. Whenever I'd ask Dad for cash he'd say: 'Do you think money grows on trees?' Well actually, Dad, no I don't. If money grew on trees I'd be gardening right now, rather than stealing it out of your wallet.

Then there was the time I made the mistake of asking Dad to

iron my shirt. 'What did your last slave die of?' he retorted. But this doesn't make any sense either. Does it matter how my last slave died, Dad? Surely the point is that he's dead. That's why I need you to iron my shirt!

My dad always used to tell me 'an apple a day keeps the doctor away'. I always thought if the doctor is really annoying you that much, why don't you just tell him to piss off? (And if that doesn't work, just get a restraining order.)

That's why when I get sick I don't go to the doctor, I just drink ten apple martinis and if pain persists I just drink ten more. I'm just glad it's not a banana a day, or these days I'd have to get a second mortgage just to stay healthy.

But it did mean I grew up most of my life convinced that doctors were terrified of apples. Like they were Superman and the humble Granny Smith was kryptonite.

I was sure if you had an angry doctor coming towards you, all you had to do was shout: 'Get back . . . I have an apple, and I'm not afraid to peel it!'

Another of Dad's classics was: 'If you stay up late, your skin will go orange, and you'll turn into a pumpkin.' Yes, but on the upside, all you then have to do is meet Peter, Peter the Pumpkin Eater and you will have a very happy life.

Don't you think that is a weird thing to tell a child? So, what you're saying, Dad, is when Mum feeds me pumpkin she is actually cooking and mashing other kids?

Food was always a theme. 'You won't grow tall if you don't drink all your milk.' (Although as a dairy farmer I always thought

Dad had a vested interest in this one.) But it is a little-known fact that most midgets are lactose intolerant.

Again, I don't know exactly where this one came from. I mean cows aren't particularly tall animals. This would make more sense if they actually got milk from giraffes.

Truth was always a major theme with my dad. 'Don't tell lies or you will grow a pimple on your tongue.' Wow, John Howard's tongue must look like the face of a kid who works at McDonald's. The pimples actually spell out the words 'non-core promise'.

I always thought it was slightly weird to try and convince kids not to lie, by threatening them with a lie.

In fact, when you examine it closely parents lie to their children a lot. 'Wash behind your ears or vegetables will grow there.' Really? I hope it's not pumpkins, I don't want other kids growing behind my ears. Perhaps I can grow some carrots, and then I'll be able to see in the dark.

In fact, maybe that's the solution for all those kids starving in Africa. Just get them to stop washing behind their ears and they'll be able to feed their entire village.

I always enjoyed shopping with my dad because it was an opportunity for him to dust off some of his classics. 'Look with your eyes, not with your fingers.' Ah, if only Winona Ryder's parents had given her the same advice.

This was normally coupled with: 'Don't touch that, if you break it, you will have to pay for it!' Which coincidentally is what Michael Jackson's lawyers say to him when he sees a kid.

And let's not forget: 'Do you think I am made of money?' No,

Dad, if I thought you were made of money I would be keeping all your toe-nail clippings and using them to shop on Ebay.

Although the other day you did say the new car cost you an arm and a leg. (Plus it would explain why you take so long in the bathroom: 'I'll be another minute son, just making some change!')

Speaking of legs, when I was going through my tree-climbing phase, Dad would always give me a bit of 'If you fall out of that tree and break your leg don't come running to me'.

Okay, Daddy Dearest, I'll try not to fall onto those sticks and stones too, they might break my bones. Maybe you can laugh at me, I have heard it is the best medicine.

Like all good fathers, Dad certainly had a lot of thoughts when it came to the area of personal responsibility.

Whenever I did something wrong I would hear: 'You're the oldest, you should know better.' Why? The others should learn from my mistakes. (Plus my brother's fake ID says he is 10 years older than me.)

I've always thought the first kid has it harder – they are the pioneer. Kind of like the first man to walk on the moon, except it's the first kid to skol a cask of goon.

'As long as you live under my roof, you'll do what I say.' Is that the rule, is it, Dad? Well technically the bank owns most of the house, so does that mean I have to do whatever the guy from the Commonwealth Bank tells me to do?

'I'll treat you like an adult when you start acting like one.' Cool, Dad, can I grab the car keys then please, I want to duck down the pub and pick up a slab and a packet of smokes?

'You have an answer for everything, don't you?' No, if I had an answer for everything I would be on *Who Wants To Be A Millionaire* now, not here talking to you. (But if you give me a couple of minutes, I can probably Google it.)

But if I ever got too big for my boots, my father would also be the first to remind me of my forgetfulness: 'You'd forget your head if it wasn't attached to your shoulders.'

Yes, Dad, you've got me on that one. I mean, how would I look for it? Maybe that's one time I would have to look with my fingers, not with my eyes.

Of course, as with most parents, most of Dad's clichés were reserved for punishment. While Graeme was always the first to 'kiss it better' when I was hurt, (fine when it's your father at home, not so fine if it's your Father at Mass) if my bawling went on too long he'd yell, 'Stop crying, or I'll give you something to cry about!' What are you going to do, Dad? Cut onions in front of me? Tell me I'm adopted? Make me watch *Beaches*?

And I knew I was really in trouble when I heard: 'Go and get the wooden spoon so I can hit you with it!' Now wasn't that the longest walk in history? Suddenly bratty kid becomes mini Hans Blix as he searches everywhere for that Weapon of Ass Destruction.

A lot of Dad's weirdest and most warped warnings seemed to involve food. 'Don't swallow chewing gum or a chewy tree will grow inside your stomach.' Yeah, okay Dad, so let me get this straight: Money doesn't grow on trees, but chewing gum does?

Or this classic: 'Don't eat too much cake, or you'll turn into a cake.' Now in Dad's defence, I suppose this is just a weirder version of: 'You are what you eat' and also goes a long way to explaining Mark Holden – he's obviously been eating too many tools (mistaking Bunnings for a Smorgy's).

But without doubt the most common warning I heard as a child was: 'Don't write on your hand in pen, or you will die of ink poisoning!' This is also the one I have the most trouble with. You see, I read the obituaries every day of my life and I have never once seen: 'Dearly departed, of ink poisoning.'

Come on, if writing on your hand was really that dangerous, criminals wouldn't use guns to hold up banks, they'd use pens. 'Get back, I have a four-colour biro and I'm not afraid to use it. One person moves and I write "Buy bread and milk" on the hostage's hand!' (Come to think of it, maybe that's why the banks chain up their pens.)

Why do parents feel the need to scare kids by inventing illnesses? Our hospital system is already overstretched; imagine if doctors also had to treat the various afflictions our parents warned us about. They'd be run off their feet treating all manner of ailments from girl's germs (medical name 'cooties') and square eyes from too much TV, to swimming within thirty minutes of eating. And let's not forget the poor boy who didn't stop 'it' and went blind.

On the upside though, it would make *All Saints* a lot more exciting: 'Nurse, get this man to surgery immediately! Not only did he pull a face when the wind changed, he then got hit by a bus and wasn't wearing clean undies. When will people learn?'

That bit about clean undies comes courtesy of my mum, Chris.

(Not that I ever understood the logic there. I'm sorry to disappoint you, Mum, but the first thing I'll do if I ever get hit by a bus is crap myself.)

Anyway, Chris was also a font of wisdom when I was growing up. I still remember the horror of being woken at 6 a.m. on the first day of school holidays by Mum shouting: 'Wake up! You're missing the best part of the day!'

I admit I did get my revenge later on when, at 3 a.m., I called Mum from the pub and slurred: 'Wake up, Mum! I'm at a party where there's free beer and I think I'm going to get a root. You're missing the best part of the day!'

I was always guaranteed a barrage of clichés when it came to my best mate, Shep. Whenever I asked Mum if I could go bike-riding, swimming or to a party with Shep, I always heard the same response: 'If Shep jumped off a bridge, would you?'

I got so sick of this, that I once asked Mum if Shep and I could go bungy jumping, just to hear her say, 'If Shep jumped off a . . . oh . . .'

But seriously, Mum did offer some very useful advice. She taught me to 'Treat everyone the way you would like to be treated' – which is good advice in theory, but if I were to follow it, I'd spend most of my time giving people sensual head massages and signed Bradman merchandise.

Mum was also very compassionate. When I was getting picked on at school, she would always comfort me by saying: 'Sticks and stones will break your bones but names will never hurt you.' I never had the heart to tell her that when I repeated this to my tormentors, not only did they keep calling me fatty-fatty boombah, they also started pelting me with sticks and stones.

(Anyway, I do believe names can hurt you – or at the very least define you. If your parents call you Sharon, for example, you are destined to work at the 8-items-or-less lane at Bi-Lo, marry Darren and pop out some pups called Aaron, Karen, and Taryn.)

But amongst the great advice, some of Mum's sayings really irritated me. Like when I eventually found something I'd spent the last few hours searching for, Mum would chirp: 'Well, it's always in the last place you look.' Well duh! If it's in the second-last place you look, or the third-last place you look, the question really has to be asked: Why on earth did you keep looking? I found the remote underneath the couch, but I was having so much fun I thought I'd check the freezer compartment one more time, just for kicks.

(Sadly, these days the only time I hear: 'It's always in the last place you look' is in the bedroom on first dates.)

Or when, in her sternest voice, Mum warned me not to suck my thumb 'or it will fall off'. I have to admit, I actually believed this one – which not only stopped the habit, it also made me very, very nervous when I started experimenting with sex.

Like most good parents, my mum was always very strict about me telling the truth. But I had to stop her once when she said: 'Don't tell lies or your nose will grow.' Don't you mean eye-brows, Mum? I mean, look at John Howard. Why is it that parents think the best way to teach kids about the truth is to tell them a blatant lie?

One of my mother's favourite expressions when I was growing up was always: 'Don't put that in your mouth, you don't know where it's been!'

It's a great piece of advice, and probably one that Paris Hilton's mum should have passed on to her.

Speaking of dating, I have to give Mum a lot of credit that girls were always welcome at our house.

Although if I wanted to stay at their place I would always be greeted with: 'You can't stay at her house, we haven't met her parents.'

Why, Mum? It's not her parents I want to drink West Coast Coolers with and then try to feel up on the couch. And to be completely honest, I'm not sure meeting someone's parents is really that much of an indication of their character.

After all, my father has never had a drink, never taken drugs, and has only been with one woman. (Yes, I'm having his share and mine.)

I often think if you really want your kids to work hard and be successful, don't bother sending them to private school. Just sit at home on the couch smoking bongs and playing Xbox. I can almost guarantee they'll become Prime Minister just to spite you.

One of Mum's other classic pieces of doublespeak was: 'I trust you. I just don't trust your friends.'

I always loved that one, because basically what she was saying was: 'I know you are an angel, and butter wouldn't melt in your mouth, but all your friends are brain-dead, drug-addled, criminal sluts.'

And while Mum definitely gave me the freedom to have fun, she also had the uncanny ability to keep me out of most trouble with a simple: 'Don't . . . even . . . think . . . about . . . it.'

Don't even think about it? Well it's too late for that, Mum. And to be honest, if I can get punished just for thinking about it, then I'm probably in a lot of trouble for what I'm thinking right now, too. And now. And now. Oh, and now.

(Although as long as the punishment is also imaginary, I'm not so concerned.)

Wouldn't it be horrible if you could get punished just for thinking about something? I'd get arrested for indecent exposure every time I read a newspaper article about Scarlett Johansson.

Try as I might, there wasn't much I could get by my mum. She would just look me in the eye and say: 'I didn't come down in the last shower.'

Of course it didn't help that I responded to that by saying: 'Really, Mum? So when did you come down then? Or are you still high? Have you been smoking that special grass that Dad won't let the cows eat again? Come sit on the couch, we can watch *The Matrix*.'

If her intuition didn't get me, then her guilt trips normally would: 'No child of mine would do something like that.' Ah, well that confirms everything I have always suspected. I knew I was adopted.

'Look, Wil,' Mum would say, 'if I've told you once, I've told you a thousand times.' Really, Mum, well if you can't tell the difference between one and 1000, can I borrow one dollar please?

When I was a kid I really wished maths worked like that. 'Yes,

Mum, I have cleaned my room. In fact if I have done it once, I have done it 1000 times.'

Speaking of cleaning my room, if I neglected it even a little I would always be hit with: 'What do you think this is, a hotel?'

Well if it is, Mum, it's not a very good one. There wasn't a chocolate on my pillow, there is no mini-bar, and when I went to school I left the 'Please Make Up My Room' sign on the door but it still wasn't cleaned.

(Although on the upside, I am glad you didn't charge me $7 for this Mars Bar.)

But above all else, the one thing that really pissed Mum off was if you ignored her. 'Am I talking to a brick wall?' Well if you are, Mum, then maybe it was the brick wall that drank all your booze and then vomited all over your bathroom.

(Of course, if I am a brick wall, when you had me you really must have been shitting bricks.)

And if you were asked a question, she expected an answer. 'I don't know is not an answer,' she would always tell me.

Although to this day I would still argue that it is a completely valid answer if the question is 'What is the square root of 456754371575575?'; 'What does it taste like to lick whipped cream off the oiled, erect nipple of a male stripper?'; or 'How do you explain the popularity of Kyle Sandilands?'

But no matter what I said, Mum always had one trump card up her sleeve: 'I hope someday you have children just like you.' Ouch, now that would be a punishment. But they would be the luckiest kids in the world if they had a mother like mine.

Despite some of her dodgier moments, I have to say I love my mother dearly and feel blessed to have her in my life. And in case you're worried that she never gets the right of reply, let me tell you about the time she came to my show, and in the middle of one of my routines, stood up and yelled: 'You're not our real son!'

❋ ❋ ❋

Like most Australian kids, I grew up watching *Play School*. Which is why I was so outraged at the recent ploy by the Gay–B–C to turn *Play School* into Gay School.

Yep, that's right. Who would've guessed that when they said there was 'a bear in there and a chair as well', the bear was a large, hairy gay man and the chair was a pouffe. The 'people with games' were playing nude tunnel ball, and the 'stories to tell' all started with, 'Dear *Penthouse Forum*, I always thought your letters were made up until . . .' And don't even get me started on 'open wide, come inside'.

What's next? Perve School? Will 'through the windows' be replaced with 'out of the closet'? Will we find out that Henny Penny used to be Lenny Penny? Will it be revealed that Big Ted is actually Little Ted's bitch? Will the craft segment teach kids how to construct their very own Mardi Gras float?

Or will there be a new *Play School* segment called 'There's something about Jemima'? I always thought it was a bit weird she wore nothing but overalls despite never working on her car – and then there was that excursion to the k.d. lang concert.

Thank God for those sensible politicians, including John Howard, who condemned *Play School*'s episode about Brenna and her two mummies. The last thing we want to be teaching our kids is respect and tolerance for diversity; it's Un-Australian.

But why stop there, boys? There's plenty more witches to hunt. What about Ernie and Bert who turned *Sesame Street* into Oxford Street; Noddy and Big Ears who lived in Adult Toy Town; Tinky Winky who looked like he was auditioning for a role in Tellytubby Eye for the Straight Guy; and of course that controversial lesbian episode of *Hi-5*? (Okay, so that one might be a fantasy.)

And let's not forget that the Wiggles are self-confessed Friends of Dorothy the Dinosaur; and with a name like Captain Feathersword, you can be sure the only thing he will be captaining is a float at next year's Mardi Gras.

But the TV-watching pollies were right. It's the Gay-B-C that is the worst offender. Not only do they pollute our screens with Gay School, they are also the home of the *Bananas in Pyjamas*.

What sort of example are we setting for our impressionable youth to have two fruits living together and hanging around in their pyjamas all day? Not to mention that with all that 'coming down the stairs', they'll struggle to get their bond back.

(Don't even get me started on that filthy woman who will be coming around the mountain when she comes; I thought it was just the yellow snow we had to avoid.)

Yes, John Howard, we must do something about their 'lifestyle choice'. It's time B1 and B2 split, stopped banana-lounging around, put on some decent clothes and got jobs.

But why stop the lynch mob there, just as we got the crosses burning? It's not only perverted sexual messages that are brainwashing our kids. There's also the rampant drug use on children's TV. *Hi-5*? Need I say more? Bill and Ben the flowerpot men were constantly stoned; Jeff won't wake up because he overdosed; and a recent episode of *Sesame Street* was brought to you by the letter 'e'.

Then there's Roger Ramjet and his 'proton pills'; Shaggy who is constantly talking to his dog 'Scooby' and eating Scooby snacks; and the Swedish chef from *The Muppet Show* who is so stoned he can't even talk properly and is permanently cooking because he has the munchies.

Do I even need to mention Mr Squiggle, who arrived in a giant bong, thought everything was upside down and was forever going on 'space walks'. And let's not forget his drugged-up mate Bill Steam-shovel – who smoked so much he now talks through a hole in his neck. And everyone knows the reason Blackboard was so grumpy: he was coming down from a big weekend. Huh-double-huh.

But that's not the extent of it. Kids' TV is riddled with lies, deceit and confusing messages. For starters, Humphrey is constantly hanging around kids without his pants on; Bob the Builder can't be a real builder – I have never seen him wolf-whistle at a passing girl or expose his butt-crack; and don't get me started on Tickle-Me-Elmo. Why that little perve wants to be tickled all the time is beyond me, but I say we leave Touch-Me-Up Elmo to hang out with rugby league players and keep him away from the kiddies.

Yep, I'm with the pollies. There should be an enquiry into *Play School* and the ABC. Maybe then we'd find out what Humpty Dumpty was actually doing hanging out at the Wall. Did he fall or was he just pissed on eggnog? And what sort of kinky shit involved all the King's horses and all the King's men?

It must be said, though, that pulling our kids in line with the 'political correctness' of our times can go a little far.

I heard recently that a school in England has changed 'Baa Baa Black Sheep' to 'Baa Baa Rainbow Sheep'. Which begs the question: What the hell are rainbow sheep? Do they provide Ken Done with the wool for his jumpers? Or maybe rainbow sheep are those that are on their way to Baa-di Gras – the rainbow being the symbol for gay pride.

Apparently in Aberdeen, they changed the nursery rhyme to 'Baa Baa Happy Sheep'. Apparently a happy sheep is one that has just discovered its owner is vegetarian, or one that has emigrated from New Zealand.

Don't get me wrong, I'm all for teaching kids tolerance and acceptance, but this seems like political correctness gone mad. (Sorry, I'm probably not allowed to say 'mad' anymore because it pokes fun at people who sell furniture at ridiculously reduced prices.)

I mean, where is it going to stop? Are we going to have to watch out for a 'rainbow cat' crossing our paths? Will AC/DC have to change their album to *Back in Rainbow*? If you like your coffee without milk, do you ask for a 'long rainy'?

Although on the upside, if this catches on, fashion experts might finally stop dubbing every new fad 'the new black' and the New Zealand rugby team will be nowhere near as terrifying when they're known as the All Rainbows.

But it won't stop there, will it? Soon we will have to ban Noddy's mate Big Ears because he might offend Prince Charles and Tony Abbott; we'll have to change the words to 'There was a crooked man' because it might piss off members of the Australian Wheat Board; and we'll have to rename Little Red Riding Hood for fear of offending men with ginger pubic hair.

We'll definitely have to get rid of Humpty Dumpty; after all, we can't be scaring kids with a story about an egg with fatal head injuries. And Hey Diddle Diddle will definitely have to go too; with all its references to violin-playing cats and cows jumping over the moon, it sounds less like a nursery rhyme and more like something Hunter S. Thompson might have dreamed up during an acid flashback.

Then there's the Three Little Pigs who quite clearly ignored all building guidelines when they constructed their houses from straw and twigs. And don't even get me started on Jack and Jill. Sure they said they went up the hill to fetch a pail of water, but we all know about Jill's waters breaking nine months later.

And do we really need to hear about Hansel and Gretel being lured into Gingerbread House when something as strange as the Michael Jackson trial can be aired live on TV?

What about the Old Woman Who Lived in a Shoe? Now this certainly isn't a story for the kiddies; if anything, it's for the attention of *A Current Affair* – or at the very least, child welfare. She had so many children she didn't know what to do. Well, how about stop having sex, you old shoe-horn? A better name for her would be the Old Woman Who Loved in a Shoe. If the stiletto is a-rockin' don't come a-knockin'.

Speaking of immoral behaviour, what about the Dish running away with the Spoon – especially since the Dish was already married, Mrs Dish had just given birth to a saucer, and the Dish had already been in trouble for trysting in the cupboard with Mrs Cup?

And don't get me started on Little Boy Blue trying to blow his horn. But we'd better not call him that as it might offend Smurfs and people who have just come out of really cold water.

And what about Rock-a-Bye-Baby? Firstly, who'd put their bloody baby in the tree-top? Yes, we know that when the wind blows the cradle will rock, but don't these idiots realise that when the bough breaks the cradle will fall, and down will come baby, cradle and all? This isn't a children's rhyme, it's a plot from *Law and Order*.

While we're talking crime, should we really be celebrating the story of Goldilocks? It's one thing to steal porridge from bears, but how would you like it if she nicked your DVD player because it was 'just right'?

And let's not forget the biggest villain of them all, Little Miss Muffet. Sure, Saddam Hussein might have slaughtered the Kurds, but I'm pretty sure he didn't chow down on them afterwards like the Terror of Tuffetville.

Yep, won't the world be a better place once the PC police re-write all our stories? Rip Van Winkle clearly suffers from narcolepsy; Rapunzel just needs a tub of Nads; Georgy Porgy is sexually confused and compensates by having an eating disorder; and Mary Mary Quite Contrary obviously has a case of ADD which can easily be treated with Ritalin.

Finally, the Three Blind Mice would be known as the Three Visually Impaired Mice; Oranges and Lemons would become Oranges and Lesbians; and Snow White and Seven Dwarves would be called Snow Rainbow and the Seven Vertically Challenged Little People . . . and we'd all live happily ever after.

Since we're on the topic of kids' education, I think it's high time we did something about our sex-ed. Because let's face it, when it comes to sex, most Aussie blokes couldn't find the G-spot with a map, compass, packed lunch and a couple of sherpas. American President George W. Bush once said Osama Bin Laden is in a place no man can find. Has anyone checked behind a clitoris?

My theory is it all stems from when we first learn about the birds and the bees (and why if Mummy bee wants to hang out with Daddy bird, she'll have to attend a few more yoga classes).

Sadly, when it comes to learning about this wonderful and essential part of life, most kids find out about sex from an older kid in the playground. At my school he was called Brother Michael.

Needless to say, this education-by-Chinese-whispers can lead to a lot of confusion. I spent most of my teenage years thinking that when Mummy and Daddy wanted to express how much they loved each other, they did something called a 'hedgehog'.

(Then again, I'm no Mr Anatomy. The first time my father put his gloved hand up the business end of a pregnant cow, I was disappointed he didn't pull out a rabbit, a dove or a bunch of flowers.)

Sure, some high schools do offer sex education programs, but when kids can learn more about sex from the latest Christina Aguilera clip than year 8 biology class, it's a case of too little too late.

For example, if you're a teenage boy who hasn't been briefed about the birds and the bees, the first time you get an erection you are likely to lose your tiny blood-drained mind. 'Oh my God, my penis is a Tranformer! Hope it becomes a bike!'

That's why it's essential we teach kids about sex at school. Let's face it, they are already learning plenty of things they will never need to know, like algebra and long division. How about teaching them some stuff that will actually come in handy later in life, like undo-the-bra and leg division?

But the course shouldn't be restricted to simple biology. It should teach the things we really need to know about sex; like foreplay, and how sometimes it's really helpful to recite the AFL ladder backwards in your head to prevent – how can I put this nicely? – being like Thorpie and having a 'false start'.

But let's talk about 'How to Undo a Bra 101', which should definitely be a compulsory unit. Sadly, most men are more capable of completing a Rubik's cube, making an origami swan, or breaking into a bank safe than removing a bra without looking.

In fact, with all the advances in science, why hasn't someone invented a bra that uses the same technology as a car's central locking? That way, you could stand on the other side of the room, press a small button, and beep beep!

But all joking aside, a course like this would be great for male–female relations, especially if it focused on the most important sexual organ of all – the tongue.

Now, get your minds out of the gutter. I am actually talking about talking. You see, I think men in particular don't talk about sex enough. Now I know some people think men talk about nothing but sex (with the occasional pause to check the cricket scores), but I'm not referring to yelling obscenities out of car windows and off building sites. I mean really talk.

Sure, blokes bang on about banging all the time, but it's always stupid stuff like: If you had to, what cast member of *The Simpsons* would you have sex with? This develops into a long, involved discussion about choosing Patti and Selma because you have a thing for twins, and whether Marge's bikini-line would be blue.

Girls, on the other hand, are a lot more open about their sex lives. To all the guys out there: I can guarantee that if you've been with your girl for longer than ten minutes, all her close female friends would be able to identify your genitals in a line-up.

And you know what? I think this is a good thing, because the only way our society will become less screwed up about sex is if we talk about it openly and honestly.

So here we go. Here's what turns me on. I love having my head touched. Yep, that's right, scratched, massaged, whatever. When I go to the hairdresser and they shampoo my hair . . . well, it's lucky for everyone I have a cape on.

My best discovery of last year was when I shaved my head. Who knew that when you're bald, random strangers come up to you on the street and touch your scalp? It's awesome. In fact, next week I might book in for a Brazilian.

But before I fall into a swoon, let's get back to the topic at hand: blokes and sex – or more generally, blokes and women.

Because if they are defeated by bras and still looking for the clitoris, when it comes to menstruation, most Aussie blokes are about as clueless as Toni Pearen trying to spell her own name on *Celebrity Who Wants to Be a Millionaire?*

A male friend once said to me without a trace of irony: 'Dude, I don't know what her problem is. All I did was go out to a strip-club with my mates for a couple of quiet beers – admittedly, I missed our anniversary dinner but I got her a card – and now she's all pissed off . . . she must have her period!'

But should we really be surprised that Australian men are so hopeless at understanding the female reproductive system? Remember, we do live in a country where the former federal health minister once compared women menstruating to men shaving. Oh yes, they're exactly the same thing . . . if you're Norman Gunston.

But if we were putting together an edition of Periods for Dummies, we'd learn as much about menstruation from sanitary-pad ads as we'd learn about farming from watching McLeod's Daughters. For starters, according to the ads, menstrual blood is blue.

Now as you know, I'm no Mr Anatomy, but I have watched a couple of episodes of *Doogie Howser*, and unless you're dating Lady Smurf then I'm pretty sure this is not the case. Where does this weird concept come from? Sure, I've heard the Queen being referred to as a blue-blood but I doubt the latest sanitary-pad ad was inspired by the Vag of Her Maj.

In fact, the only time real blood is used in these ads is when they're showing a murder victim. That's right, homicide blood is A-okay but perfectly natural menstrual blood is offensive.

Wouldn't the world be a different place if men got their periods instead of women? For starters, there certainly would be no GST on tampons. In fact, tampons would probably come free with slabs of beer, and they'd come in your favourite footy team's colours.

Men wouldn't be interested in the fancy slim pads either; for them it would be the bigger the better. Bugger sphagnum, blokes would just shove a sheep down their undies. And pads wouldn't have wings, they'd come with racing stripes, mag wheels, cup holders, and the little string would be attached to a couple of fluffy dice.

If men menstruated, Libra Fleurs would be Libra Barry's and Carefree would be branded No Worries Mates.

It'd also signal an end to some well-loved traditions. For example, I doubt Test cricket would be played in all whites. On the positive side though, I'm sure girls would enjoy reversing the sexism. 'Did you hear that George W. Bush just decided to attack Iraq and capture Saddam Hussein? He must have his period!'

But with men menstruating, we could be sure of one thing: the TV ads would be better. Instead of floral dresses, volleyball and ponies there'd be some cranky old bloke, dressed in nothing but a blue singlet, stubbie shorts and thongs. As a bead of hard-earned sweat dribbled down his forehead, he'd stare down the barrel of the camera, spit, and say: 'G'day . . . ya period, you can get it milkin' a cow, matter of fact I got it now!'

One way for blokes to learn a little about the opposite sex – and what it means when it's 'that time of the month' – is to live with a girl. Yep, since sharing a house with my girlfriend, Amy, my life has had a total makeover. (Carson, eat your heart out.)

I'd been living alone for a couple of years, and yes I really loved it. But it must be said that if you live by yourself for too long, you risk developing some strange habits.

Women who live alone get more and more cats until one day they find themselves the feature story on *A Current Affair*. Men, on the other hand, simply disregard the rules of society and morph into lower forms of life. They become the sort of people that even monkeys might look at and say, 'Dude, evolve!' In short, they turn into rugby league players.

I used to love nothing more than spending the night in front of the TV eating chocolate in my underwear. Okay, that came out wrong. I don't mean the chocolate was in my underwear.

Guys love watching TV. Remember that Channel Seven promo where the guy is walking hand-in-hand with his TV? Only a bloke would consider that having a TV is better than a girlfriend. (There are some advantages: you can turn it on from across the room, you always know which button to press, and it doesn't mind if your mates watch.)

Since Amy moved in, I've watched a lot less *Smoky and the Bandit* and a lot more *Sex and the City*. And somehow, watching *Aerobics Oz-Style* doesn't give me the same pleasure when my girlfriend is in the room.

Amy also can't stand me watching sport on TV. I got in trouble once for watching cricket when she *wasn't even home*. And I think she'd rather I had an affair than went to the football. In fact, I've had to start seeing footy behind her back. If I come home with a red mark on my collar, it's safer to claim it's lipstick than pie sauce. If she calls me at Telstra Dome and hears the cry of 'ball' in the background, I tell her I'm at a very vocal orgy.

Another thing that changes drastically when your girlfriend moves in is the amount of washing-up you do – and not just because there's two of you. When blokes are single, they eat straight out of the pan or take-away box.

Sure, one of the great wonders of the world is the Leaning Tower of Pisa, but that's nothing compared to the leaning tower of pizza boxes. Indeed, stacking is one skill blokes can bring to the relationship, especially when it comes to the dishes. To avoid ever actually drying anything, most men can stack the entire contents of the kitchen in a few racks. Come to think of it, I'm sure the bloke who designed the Sydney Opera House came up with the idea while stacking his plates in the dishrack.

But the bedroom is where things get really tricky. For starters, you have to choose a side of the bed. Where's the stress in that, you might ask? Well, my choice landed me in trouble recently when Amy read somewhere that the dominant partner sleeps closest to the door to fight off intruders. But I sleep farthest from the door. To reclaim my manliness I had to convince her that if our flat was broken into, the burglars would come through the window. (Which was difficult, since we live on the third floor.)

Also, girls love spooning, but let's be honest, guys are mostly after a fork. The reason girls love spooning is because they get front spoon. Front spoon is awesome. Back spoon, you not only have that arm you don't know what to do with, but you also get a mouth full of hair. After a night of back spoon, you're coughing up fur balls.

Another thing I've had to learn since moving in with Amy is making the bed. I've never really bothered before as I always figured I was just going to unmake it again. But as Amy said, if we took that attitude with clothes, why would we bother getting dressed, only to get undressed again at the end of the day?

Of course, living together gets even more complicated when you decide to take the next step and have children. Amy and I are not quite at that stage yet – although we do have cats which I am starting to suspect may be practice babies.

The reason I say this is because one morning when I was getting up early and trying not to wake Amy, I accidentally stepped on the cat's tail. Amy woke up immediately and screamed, 'Oh my God! What if that had been our baby? You would be the worst father in the world.' That's when I finally snapped and said, 'No, honey, you would be the worst mother in the world, because you left our baby on the floor.'

From the bedroom to the kitchen, I have learned so much about Amy – and women in general, I reckon – that I'm starting to get a reputation as a bit of a snag. So much so that the other day, a female friend asked me for relationship advice. While I was flattered, I must say I did feel like a bit of a fraud. It's kind of like asking Shannon Noll for singing lessons or getting Fred Nile to recommend a good gay bar.

You see, in my fifteen or so years of dating, I think I've learned only one definitive thing: If you want to maintain an active sex life, no matter how much your boyfriend or husband begs you, don't buy him a Nintendo. Come to think of it, rather than handing out condoms, if we're serious about preventing teen pregnancy, we should be giving kids an Xbox and a copy of Grand Theft Auto.

But anyway, a friend in need is a friend indeed, and despite being no Dr Wil, I agreed to lend an ear.

It turns out that the previous weekend my friend had met a hot guy and given him her number; it was now five days later and he still hadn't called.

Like I said, I'm no sexpert; I don't have a BA in BABES or a PhD in Pretty Hot Dudes, but I have watched almost every episode of *Sex and the City*, and even in bloke land, five days is a long time. After all, it's an entire test match.

My general rule is that waiting for a guy to call should be like waiting for a cheque to clear: If it hasn't happened in three working days then it probably isn't going to happen.

From watching late-night television (in my bachelor days), I know that girls like to sit around in the bath waiting for guys to call, but let's get serious: If he really likes you he could be sent to jail for a crime he did not commit, and he'd use that one phone call to ring you 'just to say hi!'

But sadly, in my experience, if a girl likes a guy enough she'll make excuses for why he hasn't called that even members of the Australian Wheat Board wouldn't buy.

'Maybe he was trying to wash his pants so we could go on a date, and he accidentally put his phone through the wash and lost my number.'

'Or maybe he was writing me a love song on the piano, and just as he was getting to the really romantic bit, the lid crashed down on his hand and broke his dialling finger.'

'Or maybe, just maybe, he was picking me some fresh flowers in a field when he was abducted by aliens . . . who then stole his mobile because they needed to "phone home".'

I'm sorry to break it to you ladies, but if a guy likes you enough, no amount of soggy Nokia, broken fingers or alien probing will stop him from finding you. Put it this way, if Osama Bin Laden had the phone number of a girl George Dubya thought was hot, he'd have found him two years ago.

So the question has to be asked, why would this guy not call? Well, the first thing to consider is that unless he is a balding, tubby champion leg-spinner, most Aussie blokes aren't that comfortable on the phone.

Remember that twenty-second time limit on lifeline calls on *Who Wants to Be a Millionaire?* Most men would be happy if that applied to all phone calls.

I couldn't love my dad more, but our average phone chat consists of this exchange: 'G'day, Dad, it's Wil, how you going?' 'Good mate, how are you?' 'Good thanks.' 'Good . . . I'll get your mother!'

The second, and more likely, reason is that he just wasn't that interested; but when it comes to being honest with women, most men are cowards.

I'm not proud of it, but I think there could well be a couple of girls I dated in high school who I'm technically still going out with because I didn't have the guts to break up with them. If you're out there, girls, I'm sorry . . . and happy anniversary.

In fact, if you want to understand the male psyche then you need go no further than the classic male break-up line: 'It's not you . . . it's me!'

I'll let you in on a little secret, ladies: If a bloke drops the 'not you me' bomb, it actually means one of three things:

It *is* you, especially that annoying whistling sound you make in your sleep that drives him to want to smother you with his pillow, but he doesn't want to hurt your feelings.

It's not you – and it's not him either. It's that new office temp, Jessica, who always wears a mini-skirt and long black boots.

Or finally, it's not you, it's him. In particular, his desire to get home as fast as possible so he can finish the next level on his Nintendo.

THREE

DUMB AND SWEATY

What's the deal with professional athletes getting their gear off in public?

Do you remember that picture of Michael Klim naked with a pile of fish on his groin? It was published in *Black and White* magazine during the Olympics and I still can't get it out of my mind. (I heard that Klim actually caught the fish himself using nothing but what God gave him – and a strategically placed piercing.)

But holy mackerel, what was he thinking? I've heard of someone having a case of crabs, but when you've got cod around the cods I think it's time to see a doctor/vet.

While I personally prefer my fish served without bones, in Michael's defence, perhaps he agreed to the shoot because he knows fishermen are prone to exaggeration, and he hopes one day to hear: 'You know I saw Klimmy's groin . . . and it was *this big*!'

But it's not just Michael downing the togs. Athletes from all sports seem to love nothing more than getting out of their skinsuit and into their skin.

That's why I reckon it's time the Olympics returned to its original tradition of nude competition. Having the Olympic rings on full display might be exactly what the competition needs. After all, it was Baron de Coubertin who said: 'The important thing in the Olympic Games is not winning but taking part.' And let's face it, being nude is one of the only times in life when it's better not to come first.

Think about the benefits. For starters, we'd never again have to endure the embarrassing sight of Australian athletes dressed in uniforms that make you wonder whether they mugged Big Kev's and Dr Karl's tailor on the way to the opening ceremony. (Speaking of which, competing nude would give a whole new meaning to that first night.)

Jana's knee would suddenly be the least fascinating part of her body, and what a change the post-race speeches would be as athletes thanked God, their coach, their physio and their bikiniwaxer.

A nude Olympics would also make it a lot easier to spot the athletes on performance-enhancing drugs. The finals of the swimming would be like a new reality TV show called, 'There's Something About the Chinese Women!'

And if the size of Thorpie's feet has any correlation to the rest of his body, when he 'tumbles' the entire nation might 'turn'.

A bit of sex would also draw the crowds to the minor sports. Imagine how fascinating the synchronised swimming would be if even the nipples were in sync; and if you could see our rowers' peaches and mangos, I'm sure plenty of women would fantasise about an awesome foursome with the Oarsome Foursome. (And we'd know for sure if the women's coxless pairs lived up to their name.)

I admit there would be some downsides: No one would be asked to rise for the national anthem; cyclists would have to keep dangly bits away from spokes; shooters would need to check who was around before they yelled 'pull'; and I'd have to completely avoid the table-tennis players from Bangkok.

On the track, relay runners would have to check that they were grabbing the baton; you'd have to be extremely careful when jogging with the Olympic torch; and there'd be a danger of further drug use as athletes popped Viagra in a bid to be the first across the line.

Pleasing the sponsors might also be painful as leading athletes would be forced to tattoo 'Uncle' and 'Toby' on each butt-cheek.

To some, the nude Olympics might seem like a silly idea, but in a world where sport is dominated by drugs, scandals and sponsorship deals (and that's just an average week for Warnie) people are becoming increasingly cynical about professional sport.

I was in a bar the other day and an Olympic cyclist walked in. 'Why the long face?' said the barman.

Yep, that's right, Australian cyclists were accused recently of being on the horse. Equine Growth Hormone, that is. Apparently officials first became suspicious when our cyclists asked for little men to sit on their backs and whip them.

Their worst fears were later confirmed when they realised all the cyclists had ponytails, stomped their feet at the end of each lap, and rather than Gatorade, opted for a couple of apples and two cubes of sugar following each race.

(A further giveaway was their bike-shorts. Put it this way, after a few weeks on the EGH, it wasn't only their hearts that were as big as Phar Lap.)

There was also the tragic incident of one of our cyclists getting his tail caught in his spokes. He fell off his bike and had to be put down. Well, as they say in the classics: Roses are red, violets are blue, cyclists who lose are turned into glue.

Yes, it seems if the Australian Institute of Sport were a haystack, it'd be pretty easy to find needles in it. Frankly, I'm not sure what's worse. That one of our leading cyclists was found with a bucket of syringes in his room or that the needles were discovered by housekeeping and not the drug-testers. It seems our athletes don't have a problem with drugs, but with cleanliness.

As well as the EGH, the syringes contained a banned drug called glucocorticosteroid, which suggests there should be one very simple rule for our athletes: If you can't spell it, don't take it. Unfortunately (or fortunately) this would mean that rugby league players wouldn't be able to breathe the air.

Gone are the good old days where track marks were something

you found on the track; where white lines weren't for sniffing; and where the only thing being stuck up a swimmer's nose was a rubber peg to keep out water.

While experts call for greater education and more rigorous testing, to me it seems obvious why so many athletes are shooting steroids and having a go at EPO: Sport is way too hard.

I don't blame the cyclists for dabbling in deals on wheels; I've tried cycling fast over really long distances and it sucks. You get really sweaty, puffed, and don't even get me started on chafing. That's why I own a car.

But I sometimes think the definitions of 'drug' use in sport are a bit harsh. If writing were a professional sport, I might just get caught out. Yes, I have a confession to make: my writing today is drug assisted. It's only ten o'clock in the morning, and I'm already full of Colombia's finest. Coffee that is.

Okay, I admit that hardly makes me Hunter S. Thompson (wouldn't you like to have stood downwind at his cremation? 'I'm hungry, but I don't know why!') but seeing everyone these days seems to be copping to caffeine to boost their performance, I thought I may as well get in on the act.

While some say it's all a storm in a large caramel macchiato cup, it seems professional sport is suffering from a No-Doz overdoz. Who would have imagined in this day and age when the newspaper headline read: 'Scandal, Footballers On Coke' they would be talking about the A-Cola variety?

From AFL to rugby union, players have been professing to popping pre-game pills to perk peak performance. (Try reading that sentence aloud without spitting all over the person across from you.)

Wallabies captain George Gregan said a couple of caffeine tablets could increase performance by 7% which at least goes some way to explaining what footballers mean in post-match interviews when they say 'the boys really gave 110% today!'

Unfortunately, it seems my AFL team the Western Bulldogs may have got a batch of the decaf tablets by mistake.

(And I'm pretty sure the Poms have no hope in the Ashes if they stick to their plan of taking English Breakfast Tea tablets with scone tablets, jam tablets and cream tablets before each game.)

Of course, if you really need to take caffeine tablets to stay awake, the question should be asked – how boring is your sport? Surely instead of footballers, it should be lawn bowlers and synchronised swimmers who are popping a cap of cappuccino.

While many players seem to think the practice is harmless, authorities are worried some stars might be overdoing the caffeine after there were reports their postmatch urine tests were being bottled and sold as energy drinks. Forget V, try Wee.

It is easy to spot if an athlete is using too much caffeine by examining their urine sample. If when they pee into a cup it has a white foam on the top covered in chocolate sprinkles, then it is time to cut back a little. If it feels like you are passing a kidney stone and it turns out to be almond biscotti, seek help immediately.

Authorities are also worried if high-profile sportspeople admit to taking caffeine tablets impressionable kids might copy this behaviour. Luckily these days most kids are too busy smoking, swearing, taking drugs, pouring wine over themselves or making dirty phone calls after watching Warnie to even notice.

There are even some officials who believe anything that helps aid your performance is cheating and thus should be banned. Although if you followed that logic through, they would have to ban training, and the only dietary supplement you could take would be Vitamin VB.

Personally I don't think taking tablets before the game is cheating, but it is a bad look. If athletes are going to use caffeine before a game, they should only be able to do it in liquid form. That way the extra advantage they gain in performance is balanced out by the need for a time-out toilet break and top-up every five minutes.

(Although at the rate Starbucks open franchises, it won't be long before there is actually a shop on the try line of every rugby field in the country – in between the 7-Eleven and the Boost Juice.)

Of course, it should be noted there is also a downside to taking too much caffeine. For starters, it is addictive. Sure you might start with a weak soy latte before a game, but next thing you know you are snorting lines of Blend 43 and following around the Triple M Black Thunders just so you can get your hands on those Icy Cold Cans of Coke.

And, like any drug, it can lead to harder stuff. After all, the AFL has recently had to deal with allegations that some of the players may be using recreational drugs, like marijuana and ecstasy.

Although, I've got to be honest, I think this is a different issue because, while these drugs are definitely illegal, they are hardly 'performance enhancing'. If a back has a bong before the bounce, when the siren goes he is not going to be ready to play, he is more likely to try and press snooze for five more minutes sleep. The only reason he will even chase the ball is because it has a McDonald's logo.

And if a player pops an ecstasy pill on game day I think it will be pretty easy to spot them when every time the umpire blows their whistle they pull out a glow stick; at half-time instead of oranges they have an orange Chupa-Chup; and whenever they tackle someone they just keep hugging. (Not to mention when everyone else is running a victory lap they are busy sniffing the white line.)

So, if we're really serious about making the Olympics drug-free, we should make it easier. Make the 100 metres 80 metres, and give each of the finalists a scooter.

Replace the shotput with a tennis ball, the discus with a frisbee, and make the javelin more entertaining by giving the athletes something to aim at – like the cast of *Comedy Inc.*

Want to break the high-jump world record? No worries now that there's a trampoline in front of the mat. The quadruple jump will be a breeze. (That's hop, step, step and jump.)

For those who prefer the endurance events, the marathon is now a movie marathon with the winner being the person who can sit through the director's cut of all three *Lord of the Rings* without having to give a urine sample.

And let's not forget the decathlon – or pub-crawlathon as

it's now known. In this event, competitors have to negotiate a gruelling course of ten different drinks in ten different pubs. The first to stumble across the finish-line without spewing is the winner. Now that would be a guaranteed gold, gold, gold to Australia.

In this new era of easy-peasy sport, our greatest hero would be Craig Stevens. Remember him? He's the swimmer who gave up his spot in the 400 metres Olympics final to Ian Thorpe after Thorpie was disqualified for falling in the pool. Apparently Stevens got paid $60,000 to appear on *Today Tonight* to announce his decision. Now if that doesn't make him a hero, what does? After all, he got paid not to work, which is the ultimate Australian dream.

Thinking back on the incident, I reckon a lot of people unfairly criticised Ian Thorpe's role in the whole saga. Despite having to fight vicious media innuendo that he was a 'false starter' (not that there's anything wrong with that), Thorpe behaved with nothing but good grace.

He was disqualified under rules that he accepted. He called it an 'oops' moment. Let's face it, if it'd been me, I would've used a different four-letter word.

Maturity of this sort is rare from sportspeople these days. Shane Warne would've called a press conference to tell us that his mum pushed him in.

Personally, if anyone was to blame for the pressure on Craig Stevens it wasn't Ian Thorpe, but the Australian people.

From the moment he slipped, everyone was looking for a way to get him into the race. Even the Prime Minister weighed into the debate and called it 'A real tragedy for the country.' Remember, this is a man who won't say 'sorry' to the Aboriginal people, but Ian stands on the blocks, hears someone let rip and falls in, and that's termed a national tragedy. Paging Dr Perspective!

For a moment I thought the PM might claim that Thorpe had been thrown into the pool by refugees; or follow the precedent of Melville Island and make Thorpe's lane an exclusion zone, so technically he didn't fall into the water, he fell out of the country.

Don't get me wrong, I thought it was a 'tragedy' too when I first heard about Thorpe's mishap, but then I remembered something important that reassured me . . . he can swim.

Which is more than one can say about Warnie these days. He emerges from one near-drowning incident only to be swept up in another turbulent rip. The bloke just can't seem to keep his head above water (or away from his phone). So anyway, I decided to write him a letter; an SOS, if you like.

Dear Shane, (aka Sheik of Tweak, or Horny Warnie)

Mate, firstly I just want to let you know that as a cricketer, you have no equal. Off the field though, well, I always assumed 'leggie' stood for leg-spinner, not 'leg-over merchant'. I know you're sponsored by Nike, but is this really what they mean by 'Just Do It'?

Don't get me wrong, your form is impressive, and while it's difficult to compare players of different eras, your stats would hold up in any generation, especially your strike-rate away from home. (That said, you do have the advantage of mobile phone technology. Keith Miller picked up his ladies by sending them dirty notes tied to the leg of a pigeon.)

But mate, it's getting ridiculous. We've got to the point where it's easier to make a list of English women you *haven't* texted. Actually, I can only think of one, the Queen, and that's because she has a silent number.

I've been reading your SMS smut they printed in the paper. (Filling in the bits they've blanked out is much more fun than sudoku.) Some of the messages are so steamy I can't believe your screen didn't fog up as you sent them. They should've charged you $4.95 per minute. I think it's time to admit you have a text-ually transmitted disease. What's your ring-tone? 'I Touch Myself' by the Divinyls?

Like most cricket fans, when the scandal first broke I tried to make excuses for you. Perhaps you didn't mean to send those messages. Maybe you're just really bad at using predictive text and wanted to meet those girls to 'sew'. Maybe you innocently had some 'coal' you wanted to give to their 'aunt', or hoped to 'duel' their brains out.

But even I have to face the fact that you have a problem. The only solution is to take the lead of Russell Crowe, grab your phone in one hand and throw it with full force. (Although with your luck, it would pitch about three metres outside someone's leg, and spin back in and hit them.)

Or at the very least, next time you feel like sending a dirty text, send one to yourself instead. Something like: 'UR

A DKHD. DNT HV SX WTH OTHA WMN!'

(And if that fails, perhaps you could get the good people at Advanced Hair to point their lasers at another part of your body. If the hair grows long enough down there, you might not be able to find the thing that keeps getting you in trouble.)

Or take one of those leftover Nicorette patches and put it straight over your mouth. (Incidentally, I see you're still smoking. I guess even if you only smoked after sex, you'd still be burning through a couple of packs a week.)

But as Dr Phil says, the first step to solving a problem is admitting you have one. So be a man and confess this is all your fault. I don't want to see any press releases saying: 'I didn't mean to shag every woman in England, but my mum put Viagra in my Foster's.'

Don't blame the tabloids. Sure they're grubby, but remember, you said you were moving to England to get away from the invasive press – which is kind of like Amanda Vanstone going on a diet and moving in with Willy Wonka.

You're living in a country where selling one's story to the tabloids is much easier than winning Tattslotto – and far more profitable. These days, when British women talk about their lucky numbers coming up, they're referring to your mobile.

The embarrassing stuff is sure to come out. Like the girl who claimed you sent her thirty messages in one day. Geez mate, I'm glad you're keeping your spinning fingers active, but even Bryce Courtenay isn't writing that much in a day.

Then there was the woman who alleged you stripped naked and then begged her for sex. Shane, a bit of advice: You've probably got a much better chance if you keep your clothes on right up to the last moment. Be careful when taking your shirt off – some Japanese whalers might burst into the room and harpoon you in the name of scientific research.

While we're on the topic: How exactly do you beg for sex? 'Can I have fifty cents, and a special cuddle please?'

One girl even claimed you had sex with her on the bonnet of your BMW – which, I have to admit, is a great way to get some lovin' and clean the car at the same time. Those backpackers at the traffic lights would do a hell of a lot better if they offered the same service.

She also claimed you wanted to meet her standing in the rain – which explains how you fill in time when matches are washed out – dressed as Catwoman. Warnie, you are not Batman. You are not even a batsman, you're a bowler.

Shane, mate, I know you're not the sharpest tool in the shed – over the years some of that peroxide may have leaked into your brain – so I'll use terms you can understand.

You've bowled too many maidens over, and now you've been caught on a sticky wicket, forgot to protect your middle stump and you've been dismissed. It's over. You've lost your opening partner and now you'll have to shine your own balls for a while. So stop worrying about the figures of those off the field, and worry about what's on the field. Concentrate on the one-dayers, and forget about the one-nighters.

Oh, and whatever you do, keep away from Andrew Symonds. He might get drunk one night and you'll try to shag him too.

CU L8R,
WIL J

I haven't received a response yet; perhaps Warnie did take my advice and chuck his phone into the Yarra. Either that, or reading complete sentences is utterly beyond him.

It does seem these days that sports stars are getting more and more stupid. I still can't believe that Mark Phillipoussis threw over the lovely Delta Goodrem for that scrubber Paris Hilton. Not surprisingly, this rocketed Phillipoussis to Australian public enemy number one. In fact, he became so unpopular, he was almost elected leader of the Democrats. Yep, even if Damir Dokic and Osama Bin Laden were to team up for doubles, they'd still get a better reception than the Scud.

Not that any of this comes as a shock. If anything, we're used to being let down by the Poo. His nickname may be the Scud, but a better term might be Weapons of Mass Destruction because whenever there is a major battle, he is nowhere to be found.

I admit that Delta and Mark were an odd couple – kind of like

Mother Theresa getting sexy texties from Shane Warne – so no one was hugely surprised when Mark traded Delta's Innocent Eyes for Paris's well-worn thighs. But it was the manner of the break-up that really pissed people off.

According to reports, Delta first learned that her Poo Fling was over by reading it in the newspaper. It sounds like a new reality show, doesn't it? 'From the people who brought you Surprise Wedding, it's the new hit, Surprise Dumping!'

And when it was suggested that the relationship ended because Phillipoussis's preparations for the French Open included spending extra time in Paris, well then it was Game Over.

Confused fans just couldn't fathom why Mark dumped someone as sweet as Delta for Paris Parker-Bowles. (Although the Poo does have a history of being attracted to blonde bimbos.)

While Delta was 'Born to Try', Paris is more 'Have a Try'; Delta wins Arias, Paris shouts 'Ah! Ah! Ah!'; Delta is all class, Paris just shows her arse; and while Paris has just published her first book, Delta actually knows how to read.

Now for those who think I'm being a little harsh on Ms Bangkok Hilton, when asked about the affair she said: 'I'm so happy I don't care if people say rude things.' Cool. Strap yourself in then.

To me it seems quite apt that the heiress has the moniker Paris Hilton, because just like the hotel, she stays open 24 hours a day. (Although most of the vacant space is between her ears.) You can't get room service, but womb service is available, and Paris is always more than happy to check your mini-bar.

And what is it with Paris and also-rans? First Millsy and now the Dud; next thing, she'll turn up in a buck's night video with Mark Latham. (And only 38 per cent of the country will be in favour of that, no matter who she swaps preferences with.)

Perhaps the Australian public might've been more accepting if she'd changed her name to something more local like Parramatta Hilton.

And I guess it could've been worse. Phillipoussis might have left Delta for Penelope Cruz, English rugby union player Jonny Wilkinson, or halfway through a shag with rower Sally Robbins.

Or, even worse, he could have been caught in a spa with Fani Halkia, Ionela Tirlea-Manolache, Tetiana Tereshchuk-Antipova and Sheena Johnson, the four girls who beat Jana Pittman at the Olympics. Then the Poo would have really hit the fan.

For shock value, it might've been as traumatic as when I heard all those years ago that Kim Clijsters had dumped Lleyton Hewitt. I felt so sorry for Hewitt then; I thought it would take him a long time to find another girl to love – especially one who looked so much like him.

But my heart was warmed by the news soon after that he'd chosen actress Bec Cartwright to be his mixed doubles partner for life in his new show, Horizontal Dancing with the Stars.

Apparently Lley-Lley got down on one knee (no wonder he has a hip-flexor injury; he has to stop proposing to people) and popped the question only hours after his defeat by Marat Safin at the Australian Open.

He's lucky she said yes, or it could've been the worst night of his life. (Although knowing Lleyton, if she'd declined he would have argued the call.)

And by all accounts it was a decent rock. Newspaper reports valued the engagement ring at about $220,000 although there is no truth to the rumour that he went into Tiffany & Co. straight after the match carrying a giant novelty cheque.

Initially, a lot of people poo-pooed (or 'Phillipoussis-Phillipoussised' as they say in the tennis world) the relationship, saying it was a mismatch, that it wouldn't be love-all, Hewitt was just a rebound ace, and a series of other tennis puns. (Although no one had the guts to say Lleyton wasn't the only one seeded.)

And sure, it probably would've been better for the future of Australian sport if he'd bred with another champion like Alicia Molik, Brooke Hansen or Makybe Diva.

But it seems that it's turning out to be a perfect match. After all, they are both young, blonde, rich and famous, and they've both made mistakes they would prefer to forget – Hewitt when he called the umpire a spastic, and pretty much Bec's entire music career.

If fact, things are going so well that Australia's favourite celebrity couple since Warwick and Joanne Capper recently had a baby.

Most punters tipped the bub to be called either Jennifer Love or Carmon, but in the end, the beautiful, bouncing, baby girl was dubbed Mia Rebecca. (After Lleyton's pick-up line: 'Me, ah, Lleyton . . . you Rebecca!')

But it did take them quite a while to name her. I'm sorry, but I just don't get that. You've had nine months to prepare, and you *still* want an extension?

I mean, did this child come as a shock to them? What did they imagine was going to tumble out of that tummy, a Kinder Surprise?

Apparently, the reason it took so long is both parents thought the baby was a boy; the doctor had to break it to them gently that they were looking at the umbilical cord.

Of course, all the details were published in *Woman's Day* in an agreement rumoured to be worth one million dollars – although being *Woman's Day* most of it came in recipes, knitting patterns and free shampoo samples.

But I'm pleased to say that *Woman's Day* didn't get all the scoops. Yep, that's right, do you remember the poem Bec wrote for Lleyton at their wedding? You know, the one that went on for so long by the time she finished reading it, it was their first anniversary?

Well, soon after pushing out the sprog, Bec was at it again and wrote a poem for baby Mia. After a tough bidding war with the *Trading Post*, I'm proud to say I finally secured it.

I wrote this poem for my baby Mia,
To say I'm sorry your name rhymes with diahorrea.

But we thought something classic was the best bet,
And avoided the temptation of Dennis or Annette.

We tried to be creative for the love we were makin',
And combine both of our names, but we got Relay or Bacon.

So Mia it is, and you make my skin tingle,
You're the best thing I've released since my ill-fated single.

You have the cutest little tush,
Just perfect for the Nike swoosh.

(In fact, we were going to get you sponsored,
But then I said screw it,
I didn't want you to be called
Just Do It Hewitt.)

Some ask, how do I deal with a little screaming brat?
Well, I married him, so enough about that.

Actually, Dad videotaped the entire birth, so one day you can see,
You're an extra on his new DVD.

The birth was actually pretty dramatic,
With all the screaming from the Fanatics.

Then I heard your Daddy shout,
'Are you serious? You idiot, the bloody thing's out!'

And from the high chair 'Quiet please' came the boom,
(I don't know how Tom Cruise got in the room.)

You truly are our greatest award,
So I'm sorry that Dad jumped the umbilical cord.

But he was a great support, although I was secretly hopin',
He'd stop referring to it as The Australian Open.

Sure, the birth was not easy, but then again whose is?
You're already more popular than Mark Phillippoussis.

But some memories of your birth will always linger,
Like when I looked at Lley-Lley and said: 'Hey, pull my finger!'

Then your Dad cut the cord without any jokes,
Now if he could just cut the ones to his folks.

His first words to you were: 'Gee, she's got a good head on her . . .
And thank god she doesn't look like Roger Federer.'

But he'll be a great dad, because if he does displease,
Then he'll soon be asking for New Balls Please.

A change of ends is normal for your Pappy,
But let's see how he goes when he changes a nappy.

Although his tennis should teach him a good thing or two,
He's already an expert at handling The Poo.

You see, from the minute I first met your Daddy,
I knew that I wanted him to Lley-Lley me.

When we first met, his seeding was three,
And your life began when he seeded me.

We announced you on the telly, soon after we started dating,
It's a pity you weren't born during the ratings.

But don't think we only love you because of the pay,
Or we would've had you in the Surf Club at Summer Bay.

Then if you'd been a girl or a boy,
Alf would have called you a 'flamin' mongrel of joy!'

My darling Mia, you've got a combo that never fails,
My looks and my temper, and Dad's bank details.

I'll always be there for you, even when I'm an old fogie.
You're the best thing in my life, apart from my Best New Talent Logie.

It's a gem, isn't it? Well worth all the hard-earned cash I had to throw at her to get my hands on the exclusive rights.

Okay, I admit it: It wasn't so hard-earned. I shagged David Beckham. I didn't think I had, but then I saw all the money I'd get for sharing my recollections, and suddenly it all came flooding back to me.

How could I have forgotten the texties so sexy, like Shane Warne's they should have been charged at $4.95 per minute? The romantic way he said he wanted to put his balls in the back of my net, or the constant messages demanding I get naked and cover myself in Pepsi.

I'll always remember how cute he looked when, after scoring with me, he'd pull his shirt over his head. And I'll never forget that hot night we set up the video camera and made a very special film, *Bonk it Like Beckham*.

So anyway, I decided to follow the example of Rebecca Loos and Sarah Marbeck, and sold my story to that bastion of fine journalism the *News of the World*. I wanted my tale to be taken seriously alongside all their other fine stories, like the one about the woman who was killed by her fur coat, and an article about Paris Hilton and Millsy called 'An Australian in Paris'.

Rebecca Loos' allegations ran under the headline, 'The Story You Never Thought You'd Read' which I immediately assumed was about Russell Crowe not going back for seconds at an all-you-can-eat buffet or Demi Moore making a decent movie.

Ms Loos apparently spilled the beans after she heard that Becks was texting other people: 'I thought I was special to David and the only girl in the world this devoted family man would stray for.' Which is a bit like Robert Up-and-Downey Jnr's dealer getting upset that the star was buying drugs behind his back.

Then there were claims by Aussie Sarah Marbeck (or as I like to call her: I-charge-1000-bucks-an-hour-but-I'm-not-a-lawyer-Spice) who slept with her phone by the bed for two years waiting for Becks to call. Now, unless she had the phone switched to vibrate, that does seem a little pointless. Sure, the rules of dating can be murky, but I'm pretty confident that if someone hasn't called for two years, it's not a case of treat 'em mean, keep 'em keen.

But it wasn't just phone and text messages. According to the ABC's *World Today* there were also 'audio recordings, which further embarrassed the couple' – although they could've been referring to Posh's latest single.

Speaking of which, Beckham really copped it from his wife. Apparently, the first thing she did when she saw him was whack him across the face – which is appropriate, I guess, for the slapper she is.

The reaction from the rest of the world was interesting to say the least. None of Beckham's sponsors seemed too worried. In fact, did you hear about Vodafone's new campaign: 'Vodafone, so easy to use you can operate it with one hand.'

Even more strange was that many women seemed to be on Beck's side. A common response was: 'Cool. Hope I'm next. Is there a list I can sign up to, or do I have to take a number like at the deli?'

But it's time for me to come clean with you. Sure, I'll treasure those steamy nights with Becks for the rest of my days – and the cash definitely came in handy – but the most excited I've ever been was when Adam Spencer and I interviewed the former Australian cricket captain Steve Waugh on our breakfast show.

Of course, as seasoned radio professionals of the highest calibre, we kept it Vanilla-Ice cool, but the minute 'Tugger' left the studio, we jumped up and screamed like two twelve-year-old girls who'd just caught Shannon Noll's sweat towel at an Australian Idol concert.

Now, I certainly don't want to suggest that my obsession with Steve Waugh rivals that of our Prime Minister, but when he left the studio, I did drink the rest of his cold tea.

But aside from the absolute joy of meeting one of the gutsiest and toughest cricketers to slip a plastic cup down the front of his trousers, the highlight of the interview was realising that behind his serious exterior, Steve Waugh has a great sense of humour. (After all, he does love John Williamson.)

For example, when we asked him: 'If you were batting in backyard cricket and your mum was bowling, and you got a little nick through to the keeper, and nobody heard it . . . would you walk?'

The temperature in the studio suddenly dropped about ten degrees as Steve fixed us with a steely look and replied, low and steady: 'You never walk, fellas. Makes up for that time she gave me out LBW when it was clearly going down leg.'

I knew then that Steve Waugh was the ultimate ice-man. The sort of bloke who'd stand in close to the bat, and sledge his own kids just to toughen them up. 'Hey, boys, I had sex with your mother last night!'

I was reminded of this story when, after their historic series victory in India, Australia was once again accused – this time in a book by South African batsman Gary Kirsten – of being the best sledgers in the world. (Yes, yet another instance where we are better than the Poms.)

This came as no surprise to me. After all, when most cricketers tell you they groped your granny in a spa filled with jelly, you know it's just mental warfare. But when Shane Warne says it, you probably want to check.

And the Aussies are relentless. Sometimes there is so much beeping through the stump-mic, it sounds like they are reversing a truck. Either that or the Road Runner is bowling an over.

Once again, this has led to a call for sledging to be completely banned. Personally, I think this would be a shame, as sledging has been the source for some of the greatest cricket stories ever told.

Like the time Merv Hughes responded to Javed Miandad calling him a fat bus conductor by taking his wicket and yelling, 'Tickets please!'. Or in response to Glenn McGrath calling him fat, tubby Zimbabwean Eddo Brandes replied: 'Well, every time I have sex with your wife she gives me a biscuit.' Or when Australian wicketkeeper Rod Marsh greeted England all-rounder Ian Botham by asking, 'How is your wife, and my kids?'. Or when Swervin' Mervin shouted at a hopeless batsman, 'How about I bowl you a piano, see if you can play that!'.

There are times, though, when sledging goes too far. Like the rudeness of the Aussie crowds when Australian umpire Darrell Hair accused Sri Lankan off-spinner Muttiah Muralitharan of 'chucking'. But even this incident ended positively as it resulted in one of the greatest newspaper headlines of all-time: 'Hair or no hair, Murali's balls are clean.'

FOUR

DOES MY DUMB LOOK BIG IN THIS?

Is it just me, or has the world become unnecessarily complicated lately? This really hit home to me the other morning when I popped into the supermarket for some milk.

Oh my lord, have you noticed how many types of cow juice there are in the shops these days? In the time it took me to walk past the entire fridge most of the bottles had passed their expiry date.

There's even milk which claims to be full of iron, which apparently doesn't mean when you open the carton there's a crowbar inside. Then there's powdered milk, goat milk, soy milk and coconut milk, although I'm not sure how you get that one because I have never seen a coconut with nipples.

For the health conscious there is 95% fat-free, 96% fat-free,

97% fat-free, 98% fat-free and Nicole Ritchie milk which is now 99% fat-free. Plus long-life milk, or UHT, which I think is also the sound most people make when they drink it.

(By the way, even though I grew up on a farm, I have absolutely no idea how they get the milk to be that low in fat. I imagine the farmers have all the cows on treadmills. And then another farmer takes his herd down to Starbucks for a long-black so they can make iced coffee.)

But it's not just milk that has gone option mad. Remember the good old days where the only choices you had for tea were the colour of Michael Jackson in the '70s or the colour of Michael Jackson now – black or white?

For starters, what the hell is English Breakfast Tea? I mean is it actually meant to taste like an English breakfast? Because the last thing I want is a cup of tea that tastes like sausage, eggs and chips.

(I assume Irish Breakfast tastes like Guinness and a punch in the face.)

What about Earl Grey? Well I'm sorry, but I can't drink Earl Grey. It always feels a little formal to me. Like it should only be for when you are having the Queen over for tea. It seems wrong to drink it in my tracky daks and ugg boots.

Then there's Chamomile and Jasmine (which sound a little bit too much like strippers to me), Russian Caravan (which sounds like it is strained through a gypsy's sock) and Finest Ceylon, Ordinary Ceylon and Not-Quite-Right Ceylon.

Oh, and green tea which is really good for you, although be warned, this doesn't apply to all green things. When I ate the piece of pizza from the back of my fridge the other night I was sick for days.

And don't even get me started on bread. I remember when people were impressed that we had sliced bread, in fact it was so good it became the standard measurement for how good something was.

But now, that's nothing. There's sourdough, soy, rye, linseed, soda, lecithin, wholemeal, fibre-added, fibre-deducted, thick, thin, wholegrain, multi-grain, low-grain, and the grain from Spain which falls mainly on the plain bread.

I'm sorry, but what happened to good old-fashioned bread bread?

It's not just food that's over-complicated, either. I had to buy a new toothbrush the other day. I like to get new ones regularly because I have sensitive teeth.

Really sensitive. Quite often I'll wake up in the middle of the night to find my teeth just reading the poems of Sylvia Plath, or watching movies with Sandra Bullock in them.

Buying a toothbrush used to be a relatively simple process. Now they all have fancy names like The Advantage, The Indicator and The Twister. You don't know if you are shopping for equipment to clean your teeth, or abseil down Mt Everest.

Anyway, the one I ended up getting was very, very fancy. Forget the days of the standard straight brush, mine's so bent over it looks like it should be screaming 'the bells, the bells' from a church tower.

Seriously, it looks like Mr Burns from *The Simpsons*. As soon as

I finish using it to brush my teeth, I'm thinking about taking it to the chiropractor.

And then there's the toothpaste, which raises a whole range of questions of its own: Do I need tartar control? Is my tartar out of control? And how would I know if it is, does it start making prank phone calls? You can even buy a toothpaste called Maximum Defence, which poses the question, why isn't all toothpaste maximum defence?

And to add to the confusion the toothpaste isn't just even mint anymore, it also has different flavours. It's now so confusing I'm thinking of giving up altogether and just brushing my teeth with a tube of condensed milk.

I ended up getting a toothpaste that contains baking soda and peroxide – which is handy because it means I can also use it to make a cake rise, get the smells out of my fridge, and get my hair the same colour as Warnie's.

After all that, if you think making a cup of tea and cleaning your teeth seems like too much trouble, then don't even think about blowing your nose. Did you know there are about 150 types of tissues on the market?

You can get tissues with menthol (be careful when rubbing them on your eyes, or any other sensitive parts for that matter. I discovered this when I went camping and had to substitute tissues for toilet paper), tissues with aloe vera (sounds like a British sitcom 'Allo Vera!'), and those with vanilla and a twist of lemon. Some of them smell so good, it seems a shame to use them to blow your nose; it'd be better to serve them at a dinner party.

There's even hypo-allergenic ones, which made me think that, before this, there were people who were allergic to tissues. What a horrible cycle: 'I think I'm going to sneeze, can I have a tissue? Achoo. Oh, I think I'm going to sneeze, can I have a tissue? Achoo. Oh, I think I'm going to sneeze, can I have a tissue?'

Frankly, sometimes you don't want a huge range of options. When you're standing in the supermarket in your pyjamas and trying to deal with a cold, it's one of those times.

And while we're on men in pyjamas, have you ever noticed that when men get a cold, it's never just a cold? I was sick recently, and spent every waking hour convinced I had bird flu. Well, there had to be some explanation for why I kept bumping into glass windows and crapping on cars.

It's amazing how the common cold can turn the toughest men into complete babies. I was hopeless. My sneezes were so loud, the government had to issue an evacuation warning for the area in front of my nose. One night, I sneezed so hard I reckon I travelled back in time. There were even rumours that NASA was thinking of using one of my nostrils to launch their next space shuttle.

(In case you were wondering, when I ran the tissue-purchase gauntlet, I settled on a packet of Kleenex anti-viral, which promised to kill 99 per cent of cold and flu viruses. I seriously contemplated swallowing a couple just to kill the thing off completely.)

I also noticed I became really rude to people. Especially those who said, 'Oh you've got a cold, don't give it to me.'

Yeah, dickhead, because that's just what I was going to do. I feel so great I want to share it with others. You know what? How about I get a nice Hallmark card to go with it, something like: 'Roses are red, violets are blue, I think you're a tool, so here have the flu.'

But what makes me really grumpy is that I can't believe, in this day and age, we still don't have a cure for the common cold. Our priorities are totally out of whack. I mean, we can put a man on the moon but we can't stop him sneezing all over his space mask.

Surely our boffins should spend a little less time trying to fit a camera, MP3 player and microwave into our mobile phones and a little more time trying to cure the cold? It's a screwed up world that offers more nasal sprays to give you an erection than there are to unblock your nose.

Of course, there being no cure didn't stop my friends suddenly thinking they had medical degrees. 'You've got to eat more garlic,' they advised. Well, I did eat garlic tablets, garlic mushrooms and garlic bread, but it didn't prevent my cold (instead I become completely immune to vampires and attractive women wouldn't come near me).

'Have you taken some echinacea?' No, because I don't know what the hell echinacea is. It sounds like somewhere I would go on holidays, or one of Bob Geldof's kids. (Although I've heard you can have a great time on a couple of eccies.)

Plus, I have to admit, I have a bit of a health food phobia. Isn't it a little bit suss that people who work in health food shops always look sick? Ethiopian kids must be sending them money.

And don't even get me started on naturopaths. Naturopathy must be the easiest course in the world: 'Okay, here's all you need to know. Regardless of what your patient is suffering from, just tell them to cut out dairy products and yeast. Okay, you've graduated.'

So, finally, after a week of snot, sneezing and feeling sorry for myself, I dragged myself to the doctor who took one look at me and said, 'You've got a common cold, it's going around. You should go back to bed.'

Well, thank God I got a medical opinion. If it's going around so much perhaps they should call it the 'Paris Hilton flu'.

I guess I should be grateful that the bout of flu didn't coincide with my twisted pelvis injury. Because I would've rather been forced to stand in a cell at Guantanamo Bay than be anywhere near my bed at home.

Yep, I experienced six weeks of the worst pain of my life. But even worse than the physical agony, was telling people about it.

You see, when you inform folks you've twisted your pelvis, suddenly everyone turns into Mr Humphries from *Are You Being Served?* 'Oooo, a twisted pelvis, eh? – wink, wink, nudge, nudge – how did you do that? Chasing after Mrs Slocombe's pussy?'

But I couldn't really blame them. A twisted pelvis does sound like the sort of injury you'd get from a three-day threesome with Paris Hilton and Plastic Man. (Either that, or a really spectacular diving move: 'Oh look, he's nailed the twisted pelvis in the reverse pike position!')

So just how did I get my knickers in such a twist? A failed audition for *Unco Dancing with the Stars*? A hot and sweaty lambada-off with Ricky Martin? Or did Shannon Noll finally get that voodoo doll to work?

No, sadly, I just slept wrong. Yep, I'll say that again for those of you in the cheap seats – I slept wrong. Now the question has to be asked: How bad are you when you can't even sleep right?

'Mr Anderson, I'm sorry to say you've not done well in your sleeping test. You messed up your three-point yawn, your reverse spooning was a disaster, and you were completely over the limit in Horlicks. I regret to inform you that you've failed your Zs.'

But basically, that's exactly what happened. I went to bed straight and woke up bent (which is also the title of Elton John's autobiography). I went from the Eiffel Tower – with love handles – to the Leaning Tower of Wil.

My body was fine to the waist, but then bent at a 45 degree angle. It's not the first time I've been accused of leaning to the left, but certainly the first time I could claim it on Medicare.

And have I mentioned that the pain was extraordinary? My spine was so all over the shop, teenage kids were using my lower lumbar vertebrae to play Twister. Plus I was also told I had a bulging disc (which is not a cute way to describe what happens when Matt Shirvington runs).

To cut a long story short, I spent six weeks not being able to sit or lie down. My life became like a game of musical chairs where the music never stops. Lucky I am a stand-up comic because if it were sit-down, I would've been buggered.

At least there wasn't much pain when I stood up. So I pretty much had to learn to do most things on my feet. (Everything in my office was placed at eye-level; I ordered so many phone books from Telstra they must've thought I was starting my own Directory Assistance.)

Needless to say, sleeping became a nightmare. I spent every night getting into more positions than Sting with a brand-new copy of the *Karma Sutra*.

So anyway, I finally decided to brave a visit to the doctor. After giving my back a crack and whack (I know, it sounds like a hair removal procedure) he looked at me and said, 'I have to warn you, this sort of injury can lead to sudden loss of bladder control.'

Oh great. So not only did I have a pelvis that looked like a croissant designed by a baker with Parkinson's disease, I had to control my laughing in case I wet myself in public.

What exactly was I meant to do with that information? Check whether Calvin Klein made a fashionable pair of adult diaper boxer shorts? I got so worried that I started carrying a portable DVD player around; whenever I felt the urge to chuckle I whacked on an episode of *Joey* until the sensation passed.

So what did I do to treat my bloody buggered back? Well, as anyone who's experienced the joy of back pain will attest, you reach the point of such desperation that you'll try anything for a cure. Over a period of about six weeks, I had about twenty different types of massage, and none of them had a happy ending.

Let me just say that massages really freak me out. Call me crazy, but I feel very uncomfortable being in a room with another person when they are fully dressed and I am wearing nothing but my undies. At the very least, they could tuck a couple of five-dollar notes into my waistband to relax me.

Plus they always use too much oil. One bloke poured so much oil on my back I was scared George W. Bush would invade my arse-crack. There were Greenpeace workers on my lower back trying to rescue drowning fleas.

And did I mention I'm extremely ticklish? You know that spot on a dog's tummy where if you scratch them their leg starts shaking? My entire lower back is made out of that kind of skin.

But worst of all is when they try to talk to you, especially when they are karate-chopping your back. You end up sounding like a Dalek or someone doing the traffic report from a helicopter.

But I was prepared to overcome all my phobias just to get some pain relief. So, I had physio, chiro, osteo, shiatsu, sports massage, acupuncture. I had people rubbing my butt so hard I was half-expecting a genie to pop out and grant me three wishes. I had people kneading me so thoroughly I wondered whether I hadn't stumbled into Baker's Delight by mistake.

To be honest, if I'd found a voodoo doctor who was willing to slaughter a goat for my pain, I probably would have signed up for that too. I simply wanted the pain to stop. I even slept with magnets in my bed. (All that did was pull the fillings out of my teeth.)

One thing I did learn. When seeking treatment, you must make sure you go to a reputable practitioner. I went to some great ones, but also some dodgy ones – including the bloke who gave me reiki, using an actual rake; the shiatsu masseur who rubbed my body with a small yappy dog; and the acupuncturist who thought I wanted him to fix my bike. (Serves me right for getting my medical referrals from the *Trading Post*.)

Of course, for the record, I should point out that I did seek other forms of treatment. The hippie crap is fine as long as you can combine it with hardcore prescription drugs. Yep, when my back was at its worst, I was so off my face on over-the-counter pills that cane toads started licking me to get high. I even thought of changing my name to Wil Downey Jnr.

You see, when I first hurt myself I wanted my recovery to be drug-free. But after two weeks of not being able to sleep for longer than twenty minutes at a time, I started to have visions that would've freaked out Hunter S. Thompson.

So I got a prescription. But kids, I must warn you there are a few downsides to popping prescription pills.

Firstly, you have to stop drinking – which came as a bit of a shock because when I have my multivitamins in the morning, I always wash them down with a shot of Jack Daniel's. I had to put myself on my own 12-step program, except every step was wonky and slightly limpy. (Yes, Wonky and Slightly Limpy: the two forgotten dwarves.)

Secondly, you are not allowed to operate heavy machinery. I had no intention of taking up metalwork, nor getting a job as a crane-driver. But how heavy does the machinery have to be? Was I allowed to use my iPod?

But the really bad thing about taking codeine is having to drink at least eight glasses of water a day. Of course this made me really anxious about my sudden loss of bladder control, which then threw my back out again . . . It became a vicious cycle of pain, relief, anxiety then more pain.

Anyway, my spine finally did untangle itself but my doctor recommended that in order to prevent the injury recurring, I should have regular massages.

My phobia still very much intact, I decided to take the bull by the horns and enrolled in a massage course. (By the way, I should point out I'm talking about proper massage here, the sort that makes you less stiff not more so.)

First up, I had to decide on a massage style, as these days there are hundreds of choices – everything from sports massage to achy-breaky reiki.

Initially I considered shiatsu but decided against it when everyone started saying 'Bless you' every time I mentioned the course.

I also considered Thai massage, but then I worried that it might be like the food. Sure, it's the cheaper option but half an hour later, you feel like another one.

I finally settled on Swedish massage. To my knowledge, the Swedes are famous for five things: ABBA (for the younger readers, they did the soundtrack to *Muriel's Wedding*); the chef from *The Muppet Show* who did most of his cooking with magic mushrooms; the safest cars in the world (because they are invariably owned by old men in hats who drive them at 50 in the right-hand lane); massage; and IKEA.

We should be grateful that the massage technique wasn't invented by the same bloke who's responsible for IKEA. Sure, it'd be cheaper than all the others, but you'd have to reassemble your spine at home, and despite how well you followed the instructions, there would always be one bone left over.

The great thing about doing a massage course is you're never short of volunteers to practise on. But the funny thing is they won't ask you directly. They just stand around rolling their arms as if they are about to bowl a couple of overs and say, 'Geez . . . I'm a bit stiff and sore.'

As a comedian, this has never happened to me. If people want me to tell them a joke they simply ask; they don't sit around saying, 'Geez . . . I'm a bit sad and glum' or 'My heart is so empty!'

Anyway, despite the queues of volunteers outside my door, it wasn't all smooth sailing. My first setback occurred when I was massaging my best friend Justin.

The rub was going fine until I was working on his thighs. Just like Larry Emdur on *The Price is Right*, I kept going higher, and higher, and higher . . . until, well how can we put this nicely. Unless he had a couple of week-old kiwi fruit up there, I think I may have gone a little too high. Yep, if his nether regions were a Florida presidential election, I had just encountered a hanging chad.

In my defence, it was an accident. I didn't grab Col Joye, just slightly brushed one of the Joye Boys; but it was enough to make Justin scream so high that neighbourhood dogs started barking.

I decided to put massage aside for a while and think of other ways I might benefit my fellow man. That's when I thought I'd become a registered organ donor.

Not that I think my organs are going to be worth much to anyone when I go. I can well imagine some poor sick kid getting my liver and spitting out his mum's breast to demand 'five Cougars thanks'. The way I've treated my body, when I meet my maker

I expect him to take one long look and refuse to give me back my bond.

But I do hope that when I die, my hand-me-downs might help someone else live. Or at the very least, I hope my friends use my stuffed carcass so they can drive in the transit lane.

But while Australians tend to be reluctant to donate their organs – our donor rates are amongst the lowest in the world – a recent survey revealed that seven out of ten Aussies would accept an organ from an animal in a life or death situation.

Yep, pretty soon when someone says they heard it straight from the horse's mouth they might not be joking.

But is this really surprising? Let's be honest, in a life or death situation most of us would be happy with an organ made by Benita from *Play School* out of egg cartons and pipe-cleaners.

It doesn't shock me at all that people are happy to have assorted animal organs inside them. If they weren't, the sausage and hotdog industries would have collapsed years ago.

Currently, transplants are mostly limited to pig heart valves – the irony being that it was probably the pork chops that stopped your heart in the first place. But apparently the use of other animals is not far off.

Before long, an athlete with a 'heart as big as Phar Lap' might actually have Phar Lap's heart; donkey votes would result from donkey brains; and people would be able to eat their fish fingers – once they'd covered them in tartare sauce and lemon.

While it might seem shocking to some, animal transplants do have some positives. Following your operation, you'd come home from hospital not only with a new heart, but a lovely meat tray for the family. And if the worst happened and you died on the operating table, at least the cremation would have that delicious BBQ smell.

Feeling unlucky? How about having your foot replaced with a rabbit's paw? Or even better: Why not swap your schnoz with a customs dog so you can always sniff out the person at the party who has the drugs.

Of course, there would be downsides. The dog transplant patients would run the risk of chasing cars, playing dead, and sniffing other people's bums; while those with monkey parts would notice a reddening of the buttocks and a desire to throw their own poo. (Although they could cover this by telling people they played rugby league.)

But despite all the fuss, are these animal transplants really so radical? I know heaps of people with chicken legs and butterflies in their stomach, who often come home rat-arsed and crying crocodile tears. (I even know one bloke who is hung like a horse, and he's happy as a clam.)

While I'm all for animal parts being used to save a human life, I'm not in favour if it's for purely cosmetic reasons. I was shocked to read the other day that pigs' ears are now being used to create artificial nipples.

Yep, believe it or not, many top models are getting their own nipples removed – if they are different sizes and shapes – and replacing them with the perfectly symmetrical fake nipples so they can get more modelling work.

Now I'm sorry but I don't think innocent pigs should have to go around looking like Chopper Read just because some over-paid Chupa-Chup wants to bedazzle herself with beautiful bouncy boobs.

One supermodel was quoted as saying, 'I don't think there is a downside to having a pig's ear nipple.' To which my immediate response was: When did we start allowing supermodels to talk?

And anyway, that's just crap because there are many downsides to having a pig's ear nipple. For starters, you'd have to rule out dating anyone Jewish; and if your lover pours apple sauce on your chest, you might not know if they're horny or hungry. Plus you'd have to be on permanent lookout for Mike Tyson and Russell Crowe who'd be itching to take a bite.

While we're on the subject of breasts, on the bus the other day a woman was trying, unsuccessfully, to breastfeed her child. (Well, I say child, but from the way it was screaming I was starting to suspect she'd given birth to a car alarm.)

At the next stop a sailor, in full uniform, hopped on the bus and sat next to mother and banshee. Giving it one last shot, Mum said to her kid, 'If you don't put this in your mouth now I'm going to let this nice sailor have a go!'

It seems strange to me that for all society's advances, we still have a debate about breastfeeding in public. I admit that pretty much everything I know about breastfeeding comes from the expression, 'Milk, milk, lemonade, around the corner chocolate's made', but it seems to me that women should be able to breastfeed wherever the hell they want to. (Except in cinemas, of course, because the rule that prohibits outside food should apply to everyone.)

But it seems that breasts are still a sensitive area. (Insert your own joke here.) Who can forget that controversial incident a few years back when a woman was told by airport security to drink some of her own breast milk — from the bottle obviously, not straight from the tap — because they thought it may have been a terrorist threat.

But what really confuses me is those idiots who disapprove of breastfeeding in public because they think breasts should be covered at all times.

Hey Prudey McPrude, it's not sexual, okay? In this context the breast is simply a way to dispense food; think of it as a fancy vending-machine. Sure, if the chubby, bald brat hanging off the boob was Warnie it would be a different matter, but it's a baby for God's sake.

Most of these people have no problem with breast milk per se, it's just the packaging they object to. What's the big difference between a cup and a C-cup? Instead of seeing a breast, they should just think of it as a novelty milk carton.

Look, I don't want to make a tit of myself, but I like to keep abreast of matters, and new mothers need a lot of support. So if these prudes really have a problem with a few boobs past your eyes (pasteurise geddit, I'm here all week try a nipple, okay I'm milking it now) then they should probably rack off.

Come on, is it really that big a deal to have someone breastfeed on public transport, or at the gym, or in parliament? The average person sees more breasts in a bucket of KFC.

If you want to get offended at breasts on public display, how about attacking the fat blokes at the beach? Some of these harpoon targets have breasts that would raise even Pamela Anderson's eyebrows.

Anyway, despite the bountiful benefits of breast milk, I will concede that there should be a cut-off point; a time when the milk-maid says 'Last drinks gentlemen'.

I say this because I went to school with a kid who was breastfed until he was eight years old. Now that's just plain freaky. I don't care how healthy he is, sticks and stones were definitely going to break that kid's bones.

Worst of all, his mum would actually come to the school at lunchtime – and you know how kids love to swap their lunches.

My rule would be: As soon as the child is old enough to ask for a drink, they are beyond breastfeeding age. You don't want a situation where your kid requests you eat a spoonful of Milo before feeding time so that his milk is chocolate.

Put it this way, you know it's time to stop breastfeeding when your kid asks, 'Hey Mum, can you put some milk in my coffee, please? Actually can you jump up and down a bit first, I'd prefer a cappuccino.'

❋ ❋ ❋

I've been thinking about getting a tattoo recently, but I have a couple of reservations. Firstly, I'm a wimp. I'm terrified of needles. I'm the sort of guy who freaks out if a Nanna knits too close to me on the bus.

The closest I have ever come to body art is writing, 'Buy bread and milk' on my hand – and even then Mum's warning about dying of ink poisoning rang in my ears.

Secondly, I'm concerned that while a tattoo might look great now, when I'm older and wider that cute little dolphin might look like something Greenpeace would like to roll back in the ocean.

But my biggest hurdle is I'm not sure what style of tattoo would suit me. I think I can rule out a proper 'tough guy' tattoo. You know what I mean, those blokes who look so tough even their tattoos have tattoos.

You can spot these walking canvasses at biker bars, operating the rides at the local show, or breaking your knees if you don't make the payments on your new couch. These guys have so much body art, if you stare at them for long enough, you'll see a 3-D pirate ship.

Some of the really tough ones have 'love' and 'hate' tattooed on their knuckles – although you get the impression that 'left' and 'right' might be more useful. There is only one place you can get this style of tatt, but I'm not sure I'm willing to steal a car or kill a guy just to get one. (Plus, with my luck, I'm likely to lose a finger in an accident and spend the rest of my life explaining why I have 'love' and 'hat' on my hands.)

So if the tough-guy tatt is in tatters, the next option would be something symbolic, like a Chinese or Japanese symbol that sums up your attitude, or expresses something that's really important in your life. In my case though, I doubt there is a Japanese symbol for doughnuts.

My only fear is I'll get a tattoo artist who doesn't like me, and instead of my star sign, my lower back will feature the Japanese words for 'Caution, Wide Load'.

I could go the popular choice and get my partner's name tattooed on me, but this is very risky. Johnny Depp had to change his 'Winona Forever' to Wino Forever when that relationship went belly-up. (Perhaps that's why J-Lo keeps her bum so big; she has to make room for all her exes.)

Even worse, Rod Stewart's daughter Kimberley had her boyfriend's name tattooed near her groin – and then he promptly dumped her. (Although many guys I know would be willing to change their name by deed poll to help her out.)

Surely if you are going to get a tattoo on your groin, the safer option is your own name. That way, if you have a lot of one-night stands, your current partner would know what name to call out at the height of passion.

My girlfriend's name is Amy, and although I hope we'll be together forever, I do worry that if we ever did break up, I'd spend the rest of my life explaining my 'Amy Forever' tattoo. 'Oh no, it's not another girl, I'm just a very big fan of their comprehensive car insurance policies.'

David Beckham went the safer option and was tattooed with his children's names. Perhaps if he also got Posh across his fingers, he might remember her next time he sends a text message.

Above all else, the main reason I haven't got a tattoo is my appalling fashion sense. I'm someone who once thought wearing a hyper-colour shirt with tight acid-wash jeans was the height of *prêt à porter*.

But at least you can give a shirt to the salvos when it goes out of fashion – although I suspect there are even homeless people who'd turn up their noses at my Wham 'Choose Life' T – when it's your arm it's a whole different story.

I'm scared skinless I'd choose something I thought was incredibly groovy, but would be out of fashion before the ink dried. So if I do take the plunge you can guarantee I will have thought it through.

Which is something I wish I'd done before getting my hair cut recently. Seriously, people keep asking me if I lost a bet. Either that, or was I attacked by an epileptic Edward Scissorhands? My hair is so bad even Andrew G could take the piss out of me.

Okay, I might be exaggerating, but on a scale of dodgy noggins it's definitely up the Ray Martin end. While we're on the topic, what is going on with Ray's do? He looks like a fully-grown Lego man. Is that hair on his head or a helmet? It's as if his stylist grabbed a stack-hat, painted it black, and then finished it off with a coat of lacquer before popping it on Ray's head. (That must be why Channel Nine sent him to cover the tsunami – he's completely waterproof.)

Some people have the personality to pull off a desperately dodgy do – like Tony Santic, the owner of Makybe Diva. 'Hey Tony, John Farnham called from the '80s, he wants his mullet back!' Here's something for free: When your mane is longer than your horse's it's time to get a trim.

But back to me. My problems started when I looked in the mirror and realised I was desperately in need of a haircut.

The main issue with my hair is that when it hasn't been cut in a while, it becomes really thick. Yep, if my hair had a personality it would be David Beckham.

And it grows really, really, really quickly. In fact, my entire scalp is made up of the same hair as John Howard's eyebrows. I have more new roots a month than Warnie.

It's the sort of hair you don't so much trim as back-burn. Luckily, I've never had nits, but the Blair Witch was living in there for a couple of months.

To make matters worse, as soon as it gets long, it also gets curly. It's as if someone is secretly feeding me bread-crusts in my sleep. And if it gets even a little bit humid outside, I start to resemble the love-child of Mike Whitney and Dickie Knee. (Don't even get me started on the short and curlies on the back of my neck; from behind I could be mistaken for Guy Sebastian's bikini-line.)

So I rang my usual hairdresser, only to be told he was away and I would have to see someone else. This was very bad news, for four main reasons.

Firstly, I hate seeing other hairdressers. It makes me feel like I'm having an affair. Secondly, I have a long history of hair disasters — although this might be because I tend to choose hair salons on the quality of the pun in their name rather than on their qualifications and reputation. Over the years I've had my hair done at His and Hairs; Hair Majesty; Lunatic Fringe; Right Hair, Right Now; Head Master; Curl Up and Dye; Avon Curling; The Perminator; The Best Little Hair House in Texas; Perms of Endearment; Good Head; and my personal favourite, The Bald and the Beautiful.

Third reason I hate going to a new hair salon is time. My usual hairdresser can get me in and out in less than sixty minutes, but when I rang to book at the new place they said, 'Make sure you allow three hours.'

Three hours? I don't even do anything I *like* for three hours. Surely I should be able to get my hair cut in less time than it took for Frodo and Sam to find the ring?

Three hours? Test match cricket doesn't even take that long. If I am going to be there for three hours, I don't just want a cup of tea, I want a meal and a movie.

Three bloody hours? Even on a practical level, at the rate my hair grows, by the time they get to the end, the hairs they cut first will have already grown back.

And finally, the main reason I hate going to a new hairdresser is the price. Because I'm a regular, my usual guy gives me a tidy discount, but this time I'd be up for the full cost. I'm no tight-arse, but I think haircuts are getting too expensive when you have to put them on lay-by. If I'm going to pay 150 bucks I want every single hair cut individually. And I don't just want a head massage, I want a happy ending too.

Seriously folks, for $150 I could get the bloke from Jim's Mowing to do my lawns and then take a bit off the back and sides with the whipper snipper. Let's face it, it couldn't look any worse.

My self-esteem at an all-time low, I sank even further when, sitting in a cab listening to talkback radio the other day, a caller rang in and said: 'Morning, John, long-time listener, first-time caller. John, I was watching the ABC last night, and I saw that show *The Glass House.* That host is not only unfunny, but also the ugliest man on Australian television.'

Now that's harsh: The Ugliest Man on Australian Television. Forget the Logies, she wanted to nominate me for the Uglies! In a world where they allow Kyle Sandilands on TV with a hairstyle that resembles the Opera House, that really hurt.

Didn't she ever catch an episode of *Beauty and the Beast* hosted by Stan Zemanek? He had a face like a bashed-in biscuit tin. That bloke fell out of ugly tree and hit every branch on the way down. Stan's the bloke Chopper Read stands next to at parties so he can look good in comparison.

And in case you think I'm having a go at David Koch from *Sunrise* – I mean, you've got to love a bloke who brings a touch of the dodgy uncle to breakfast television – even he sometimes looks like Harry Potter after a thirty-year pub-crawl.

Maybe it was my teeth that so offended her? Look, I'm the first to admit that my pegs go off in so many different directions, you'll assume my dentist is one of the druids who built Stonehenge. Even the *Karma Sutra* has less angles than what's in my mouth. One of my incisors is so crooked it has just been appointed to a vacancy on the NSW Supreme Court.

That's why I was horrified to realise recently that it was time for my six-monthly dental check-up. Because whether it's going through customs at the airport or visiting the dentist, I hate nothing more than having my cavities checked.

Yep, forget the electric chair, it's the dental version of the Smoky Dawson recliner that fills my heart with fear. To me, the waiting room resembles a scene from Decayed Man Walking.

Seriously, is there any worse place on earth than sitting in a dentist's reception listening to the drilling from next door? (Not to mention that horrible sucking noise, which makes me wonder whether Paris Hilton has popped in. Either that, or they are making cappuccino.)

Of course, it's even worse once you get into the room and notice that the dentist's drill is so big you wonder whether he is about to start constructing an in-ground swimming pool. Rather than a dental nurse, assisting him should be a council worker holding a Stop/Slow sign.

And why is it that dentists always wait until your mouth is completely full of machinery and cottonwool before they strike up a conversation? It's hard to keep your cool when you sound like a cross between Sylvester Stallone and Ozzy Osbourne.

Then they ask you to spit, but by this time your mouth is so swollen, the best you can do is drool and slur. I'm starting to wonder whether the Swedish chef from *The Muppet Show* wasn't Swedish at all, he'd just undergone some major dental work.

On the upside, my fear of dentists has always frightened me into taking very good care of my teeth, especially for someone who grew up in the country where generations of in-breeding means that if you have more teeth than fingers, you're pretty happy.

Seriously, some of the kids I went to school with had cavities so big if you spoke into their mouth you'd hear an echo. Their teeth had more gaping holes than an M. Night Shyamalan film.

The only part of my dental regime I neglect is flossing. Each time I visit the dentist he gives me the big speech about the importance of flossing, and each time I follow his instructions for about a week following my visit. Before long, I am back to my old habits and the closest I get to a floss is getting a Snakes Alive lolly caught in my teeth.

Sadly, this also means that when my next dentist appointment comes around, I try to cram six months worth of flossing into about two days, so my teeth are not only dirty, but I turn up with rope burn on my gums.

I must admit though that the one thing I do enjoy about the dentist is the gas. I love that nitrous oxide. How cool would it be to strap a tank of it on your back before going to a rave.

I hear a lot of people only get the gas for major operations. I get it for everything, from getting my teeth cleaned to paying the bill (which, let's face it, is still the most painful part of the process).

In fact, I suck in so much nitrous oxide, my dentist once suggested that he wear the mask while he fills the whole room with gas.

Being on the gas is a little like being hypnotised – a bit drunk, a bit high. In fact, if I can't get hold of a tank of the stuff before my next rave, I might just take a hypnotist with me – although people might wonder why I'd cluck like a chicken every time a bell rang.

Now, I don't know how many of you have had the experience of 'going under' but it's pretty freaky.

You see it all started when a radio program invited Tamsyn Lewis, Liz Ellis, Fatty Vautin, Ian 'Dicko' Dickson and myself to be hypnotised. (I know, that's so many C-grade celebrities, we could've been starring in a Channel Nine reality TV series.)

Peter Powers was the name of the world-famous man who was going to put us under. (And let's face it, with a moniker like that, just as well he's a hypnotist. What a waste it would be to hear, 'Hi! I'm Peter Powers, your Subway Sandwich artist.'

I'd always assumed that while hypnotism may well be effective, it only worked on people with weak minds – like Scientology, or extended warranties. Suffice it to say, many of my preconceptions were challenged that day.

I was the first to go under, and that's when the fun started (at least for everyone else). Peter kicked off with an easy one. He made Dicko and me believe we were smelling a really bad odour – and I'm talking *really* bad. I could actually feel it in my nostrils. Think Warnie's jock-strap after fifty overs and a meal of baked beans on toast.

Then he really began to mess with our minds; he took me back to when I was eight years old. I found out that I wanted to be a fireman when I grew up, and my worst fear was Michael Jackson.

I then ran across the room, skolled a tray of drinks, burped into the microphone and told the female co-host she had nice boobs. I was starting to wonder whether Mr Powers hadn't turned me into a rugby league player.

Suitably warmed up, that's when the really embarrassing stuff started – the dancing and singing. Now it should be pointed out that when I dance, people try to roll me on my side and hold my tongue because they think I am having a fit. With Dicko and I shaking our substantial rumps, it was like an episode of Dancing with the Chubby Unco Stars.

And if my dancing is bad, well my singing is even worse; so imagine my shock when Dicko and I stared into each other's eyes and crooned, 'You've Lost That Loving Feeling'. This is when I really understood the true power of hypnotism, because if Peter Powers could bring me and Dicko together then get him over to the Middle East.

But at this beautiful moment things took an ugly turn. I realised that my penis was missing. Peter told me someone had stolen mine and replaced it with a smaller, shrivelled one. To my horror, when I looked down my worst nightmares were confirmed. If it was a fish, you would have thrown it back in. There never was a more intense game of Where's Willy.

Thankfully, when I woke up a few minutes later, everything was back to normal. Apart from the scare, I must say that I enjoyed the whole experience. (And not just because doing something embarrassing for a few minutes and then falling asleep reminded me of my early love-life.)

For one thing, it challenged many of my assumptions. For example, it turns out that Dicko is not a tool after all, but a really great bloke with an excellent sense of humour. Not only did that mess with my mind, it also buggered about half of my stand-up material. After all, what if Dannii Minogue is talented? Maybe Russell Crowe isn't a dickhead, and maybe, just maybe, Daryl Somers is actually funny.

❊ ❊ ❊

Could the power of hypnosis just be a really cool mutation? I was watching the new X-Men film the other day when it suddenly dawned on me – I think we're all born with mutant powers, it's just that some of them are much cooler than others.

Sure, I might not be able to make people embarrass themselves in public just by the power of my gaze, or do an Edward Scissorhands impression when I get angry like Wolverine, but I do have the uncanny ability to always choose a perfectly ripe avocado.

(Although I must confess, that skill is not as handy in fighting crime, unless you are going up against the evil Supreme Nachos Man. Holy guacamole!)

The US might not be able to find Osama, but if he was holding the only ripe avocado in Afghanistan and I wanted to have salad, I'd be able to find him by dinner.

It's a gift. When my mates buy avs they are either so hard you could open the bowling with them, or so soft even an Ugly Dave Grey nasal spray wouldn't help.

But me, if I were a native American my name would be Dances With Avocados. (Which I can pretty much guarantee would get me beaten up by all the other Indians, especially Punches With Fists and Gives Big Wedgies.)

Anyway, all this mutant talk got me thinking about two things. First, that I could really go some avocado on toast, and secondly, if I could choose any superpower what would it be?

I'm guessing a lot of people would probably go with the

predictable ones, like being able to fly or see through people's clothes, or fly over people and see through their clothes.

But not me. I'd like a more practical power. You see, I have an Apple computer, and there's one command I use more than any other, Apple-Z.

For those who don't use Macs, Apple-Z undoes your last mistake. It's the best thing ever, no matter how many times you stuff up, all you have to press is Apple-Z and it's like it never happened. (And it's heaps easier than trying to apply liquid paper to a computer screen.)

So I started thinking, wouldn't it be great if you had that power in real life? That's right, I want to be Apple-Z Man!

Imagine the scenario, a man is shopping with his wife, and everything seems normal until danger strikes: 'Honey, do you think my bum looks big in this dress?'

Without thinking he falls into her trap: 'It's not the dress, love, your bum would look big if I looked at it through the wrong end of a telescope. Maybe you should get the dress in white and they can use you as the sightscreen at the SCG . . . oh dear God, what have I done, help me, Apple-Z Man.'

There's certainly a few times in my life where I would have loved a visit from Apple-Z Man. I could have definitely used him in the supermarket the other day when I went to give my girlfriend a massive bear-hug from behind . . . unfortunately, it wasn't my girlfriend.

Or when I was 18 and at a bar, and decided to try one of my very best pick-up lines on a very hot girl. I went up to her and said: 'Is your Dad a thief?' She just looked back at me and said: 'No, but he is a murderer, and he will be here in a couple of minutes.' Help Me, Apple-Z Man.

Then there was the time I met one of my comedy heroes, Lenny Henry, when I stood next to him at the urinal at the Montreal Comedy Festival.

Now, a normal person would have waited until we were done before saying anything but, clearly, I am not a normal person. I looked over and said: 'G'day Lenny, I'm a huge fan!' He looked back over to me, then down, and said: 'Not that huge!' Help me, Apple-Z Man.

And I could have done with him again a couple of minutes later when I asked Lenny if there was anyone he had been excited to meet, and he said: 'Muhammad Ali, I was so nervous my hands were shaking,' and I spurted out: 'Well you wouldn't have been the only one!' Help me, Apple-Z Man.

Then there was the time when I nearly got sacked on the spot on national radio after running through shows I would like to see having 'Uncut' editions, and tried – unsuccessfully – to say the show title Rex Hunt Uncut. Help me, Apple-Z Man.

And Apple-Z Man certainly would have come in handy when I was doing an extremely important audition gig in New York and I only had five minutes to showcase my set in front of some high-powered producers.

Unfortunately, in the middle of my routine three people came in late and sat in the front row of the audience. The first was the tallest man I had ever seen – I thought he had dandruff, it was snow – the second bloke was average height, and third guy was so small even Oompah Loompahs would hang shit on him.

Now, a professional would have just kept going with his set but, clearly, I'm not a professional. I just looked down and said: 'Let me guess why you were late, your porridge was too cold . . .' Help me, Apple-Z Man.

FIVE

BIG DUMB WORLD

In a taxi, on the way to the airport for an overseas trip, I finally worked out why the world is so screwed up. All the politicians are brain-dead, corrupt morons who wouldn't know their policies from their private parts, and the people who really know how things should be run are driving cabs.

Well, that's according to most cab drivers I meet. I guess it's my own fault for sitting in the front seat. Everyone knows if you don't want to talk, it's back seat only. But I don't like to feel I'm being chauffeured around.

I know it's silly, but at least if I sit in the front I can pretend I'm getting a ride from a mate, and I just slip him a couple of bucks for petrol at the end.

(Admittedly, I don't have too many friends who drive bright

yellow cars with their phone number on the side, don't know where my house is, and think Elton John 'just hasn't found the right girl yet'.)

Anyway, I catch cabs often – that's what happens when you drink with breakfast – so I've compiled a list of my worst taxi offences.

First is the cab driver who doesn't know where he's going. Now I'm not suggesting that cabbies should know where everything is (even God misplaces Guam occasionally) but there's nothing worse than getting into a cab at the airport and being asked for directions.

'Well, no mate, I'm sorry but I don't know where I am, I barely speak the language . . . hell, I don't even know what side of the road you drive on here. What's that, would I like a job as a taxi driver?'

Look, I have absolutely no problem with a cabbie having to look up an address. I'd just prefer it if he did so before he started the meter rather than halfway through the trip – and then hand me the street directory and ask me to do it.

'Dude, I'm not your navigator. This is not *The Amazing Race*. Would it make it easier if I drove too so you can have a snooze? Although I'll expect you to sling me a couple of bucks at the end of the trip, and sorry no, I don't have change for a twenty.'

Then there's the cab driver who knows the most direct way, but chooses not to take it. 'Hey mate, I'm no Mr Melway, but I'm pretty sure the most direct route to the Sydney Harbour Bridge is not via the MCG and Federation Square. Here's an idea cabbie, how about you ask that bloke you've been chatting to throughout the trip if he knows the most direct way?'

Yep, it never ceases to amaze me that taxi drivers don't make it onto those annual lists of the most desirable men. Everyone knows how much the ladies like a man in uniform, even better surely, is one who never goes for the quickest route. (Although like most guys, they still have trouble finding the exact spot.)

Anyway, regardless of how bad the service is, I always tip taxi drivers – especially if I have a Cabcharge docket; then I'm signing cheques like Eddie McGuire on *Who Wants to Be a Millionaire?* – partly because I reckon taxi driving is a tough, thankless job, and partly because I hope they might spend some of that extra cash on deodorant. I know most cab drivers smell like angel farts, but have you ever got into a smelly cab on a really hot day? Hey boys, I like garlic sauce as much as the next guy, but you're meant to eat it not bathe in it. Try and pick up Calvin Klein next time you are cruising for a fare.

Come to think of it, that's probably why those plastic bubbles were installed – to keep the smell in. Those pine air-fresheners blocking the windscreen would be better off in your armpits, Mr Cabbie. I mean, I know it's called a taxi rank, but really . . .

In their defence, taxi drivers do have to put up with some real crap from passengers. If cabbies had a dollar for every time someone asked, 'Have you been busy tonight, mate?' they might have change for a fifty.

And then there's the drunks. From the rugby players who've mistaken the cab for a clown car and are trying to cram fifteen people into four seats, to the idiot who opens the door and says, 'Do you have room for a slab of beers and a kebab' and then vomits in the back seat, it's no wonder cab drivers hide inside their plastic bubbles.

That's why it's great when occasionally you get a cab driver who restores your faith in the entire profession. It happened to me just the other day when I hailed a taxi that was – and I swear this is true – towing a caravan.

It was the most Australian thing I've ever seen. Turns out, he was going on holidays and figured he may as well make some money on the way. His family were in the van, and he was taking fares, but only if they went in the direction of the Gold Coast.

Anyway, after a few wrong turns, I finally made it to the airport just in time for my flight to New York. But of course that's when the fun and games really started – at customs.

God, all that paperwork is enough to drive you barmy. I absolutely *hate* filling in forms, it makes me feel totally dyslexic. (Which, incidentally, seems a really tough word for dyslexics to spell.)

For some reason, I always end up writing the wrong answers in the wrong boxes; so under birthday I will put 'male', and then under sex '31 January' – which makes it seem like that was the last time I got any.

But the biggest challenge is resisting the urge to write joke answers to questions such as: 'Do you have a physical or mental disorder?' (Which, ironically, seems to be a good enough reason for the Australian immigration department to deport people.)

What exactly do you mean by 'physical disorder'? I have a really bad case of man-boobs, but in the US that should mean I fit right in.

And how do you define 'mental disorder'? Would Crazy John be allowed to visit the States, or are you only deemed ineligible if you eat the pencil and write 'I am a cow' in blood?

This is followed by the even more personal question: 'Do you have a communicable disease?' Is this a customs form or one for speed-dating? 'No I don't have any diseases, and I also enjoy banjo music and sex on the beach – both the activity and the drink.'

It's a weird question, isn't it? I'm always tempted to write, 'Well, I don't now, but if all goes well, I might come home with a few.'

The next question is even more difficult: 'Have you ever been arrested for a crime involving moral turpitude?'

What the hell is moral turpitude? I've never seen Ice T on *Law and Order* say, 'Yo, this bro is goin' down for moral turpitude. I'm gonna bust a cap in his ass!'

It actually sounds like a communicable disease. 'I'm sorry, sir, you have a bad case of moral turpitude, but if you use this cream twice a day it should clear right up.'

It's at this point the questions become really ridiculous. 'Are you seeking entry to engage in criminal or immoral activities?' Isn't it great that with all the extra security, we still rely on the honour system?

Can you imagine the master criminal answering, 'Well, yes I was. I was going to rob a bank and kill innocent people, and maybe even fit in some moral turpitude. I know I shouldn't be admitting this, but my mum warned me to never lie.

'By the way, if you are interested, I have attached a detailed copy of my plans, included a list of accomplices, and also some evidence about the assassination of JFK. And while we're at it, in grade 6 I borrowed a copy of *The Magic Faraway Tree* and never returned it.'

How do you define 'immoral activities'? I'm not planning to covet my neighbour's ass, but if you are talking sex, drugs and rock'n'roll then sure, do you have the numbers of anyone who can help me out?

This is followed by the even more hilarious: 'Have you ever been involved in espionage or sabotage?' I have to stop myself from writing, 'I could tell you, but then I would have to kill you.'

And finally: 'Are you involved in terrorist activities?'

Has anyone actually answered 'yes' to this question? Surely if you are trained as a terrorist agent for Al-Qaeda, the IRA or the CWA, the first thing they teach you at terror TAFE is never tell anyone about it. And to get rid of that badge, 'Become a suicide bomber now, ask me how.'

If this question proves effective, perhaps they should go the whole hog and ask: 'By the way, do you know where Osama is?'

I finally made it onto the plane and some thirty hours later – which felt more like a lifetime – I arrived at my hotel in New York.

One of the best things about the life of a stand-up comedian is the hotel mini-bar. There is nothing I love more than coming back after a gig, cracking open a tiny bottle of vodka, a mini-can of lemonade and a fun-sized Mars Bar, and pretending I'm a giant.

But why is everything so damn expensive? They've halved the sizes, but doubled the price. I'm convinced the people who devised the food prices at airports, the footy and the movies are also responsible for the nation's mini-bars.

Forget petrol prices, it's time for the ACCC to launch an investigation into Mr Pringle when a small tin costs five dollars. And six dollars for a bottle of water? If Jesus returned, he'd turn wine back to H_2O and make a profit.

Put it this way, if you are about to go to England and want to get used to the exchange rate, just book yourself into a hotel room for a couple of weeks.

Oh, and while I'm going all Osh-Gosh-David Koch and dispensing financial advice, never – and I mean never – make a long-distance phone call from a hotel room. You can call 0055 numbers that cost less per minute than the average hotel phone rate.

So why is everything so steep? My theory is it's because the first thing anyone does upon entering a hotel room is steal everything.

And I mean everything. Tea, coffee, shampoo, conditioner – suddenly we're all Winona Ryder. Before you know it, you are drawing up elaborate plans to fit a sofa-bed into your overnight bag.

Remember that footage of Iraqi looters loading TVs and air-conditioners onto the back of their donkeys? That's me on the in-house security tape every time I leave a posh hotel.

The worst thing is, I don't even want the stuff. I have so many unopened shower caps, shower gels and novelty soaps, I'm thinking about opening a Body Shop.

That said, I do think some hotels go a little over the top when guarding against theft. At one place I stayed in, they had chained the remote control to the bedside table.

Okay, my first question is: Who'd steal the remote control? My couch at home has so many remotes it looks like the command desk of the Starship Enterprise. Who needs one that won't even work? And question number two: Doesn't chaining the remote to the bedside table work against the whole idea of it being a 'remote'?

But there is definitely something intoxicating about hotel rooms that makes you do things you'd never dream of doing in your regular life. Five minutes after checking in I'm moisturising, I'm getting a massage, I'm going to the gym, I'm even using the sewing kit.

You know what else I absolutely adore for no good reason? The way they fold the toilet paper so it makes an arrow at the end. Yep, these days to be a hotel cleaner you have to take a course in Origami for Dummies.

(Some hotels even go the extra step and put a paper sash across the toilet-seat so you can pretend your toilet has just won the Miss Universe pageant.)

Oh, and then there's the bed-sheets. How do they tuck them in so tight? They are tauter than the skin on Cher's face (although not quite as many men have slept in them).

But without doubt, the most important item in any hotel room is the Do Not Disturb sign. Especially when showering. I reckon the hotel staff of this nation have seen me naked more times than my girlfriend. It must be said that the most intimate moment of a romantic weekend should always be accompanied by cries of, 'Yes, yes, I love you' rather than 'Housekeeping!'

Of course, hotel life is not all a box of ridiculously overpriced chocolates. For starters, there's the annoying elevator swipe-card that makes travelling in the lift more difficult than hacking into the Pentagon – especially when you're drunk. And then there's the one minute free preview on the movie channel – not long enough on the adult channel, a little too long if the movie stars Ben Affleck.

But for me the worst thing about staying in a hotel is having a porter carry your bags. I know it might seem weird, but it makes me feel uncomfortable. The only way I can justify it is by pretending they're a mate helping me move. 'Okay, you can carry my bags for me . . . but you have to let me wash your car in return.'

Are you meant to tip them? I never know what's appropriate. 'Here are a couple of shopper dockets. This one gets you two-for-one at Pizza Hut!'

Of course, if hard yakka is what you're after, you can always go camping.

I'm sorry, but I just don't see the appeal of spending an extended period in a tent, unless it's trackside at Flemington and chock-filled with *Neighbours* starlets.

As a man who has chosen a life of indoor work with no heavy

lifting, I find erecting a tent about as difficult as George W. Bush trying to speak English.

Usually after about an hour I still don't have anywhere to sleep, but I've managed to construct an entire IKEA outdoor dining set.

Then there's the lack of room. As my girlfriend and I are hardly Mike and Mal Leyland, we normally borrow a tent so small that once inside we resemble a poorly made sausage roll. It's less like being in a tent, and more like a return to the womb. If we move around it looks like Anna Nicole Smith jogging in a tube-top.

And then there's the added challenge of trying to fit the tent back into the bag at the end of the trip. It's like Kim Beazley trying to climb into Thorpie's bodysuit.

And don't even get me started on the bedding. Put it this way, if air-mattresses were comfortable, people would sleep on them in their homes; air-conditioning is more to my taste. The only time I'll sleep on an air-mattress is when I live in a bouncy castle.

And have you ever got a bug trapped in your tent? Sounds like someone is trying to land a helicopter. At every camping trip I've been on, there are more bugs than ASIO has installed at David Hicks's place.

I'm an animal-lover and in principle, I disapprove of killing them, but if baby seals buzzed in your ear all night, I'd club them to death too.

And as for the bathroom – let's not go there. Normally I get freaked out when the toilet doesn't have half-flush and full-flush. But digging a hole in the ground? I'm sorry, I'll do that only if

I have to bury a body. If I do dig a hole, next year I want to be allowed to march on Anzac Day.

Basically, I believe that camping is an insult to evolution. What next? Shall we start climbing trees and slinging poo at each other? I just don't get the fun of pretending that I don't have a house. If that's your idea of a good time then why not go the whole hog and live in a cardboard box on the street?

'Ah, I had the best weekend, I was totally homeless. I slept on concrete, ate garbage, and went to the toilet in my pants . . . it was just really good to get away from it all.'

I'm just not the outdoors type. My idea of slumming it is a hotel that doesn't have 24-hour room service. If I want to rough it, I buy recycled Home-Brand toilet paper. Seriously, when it comes to the great outdoors I make Carson from *Queer Eye* seem like the Crocodile Hunter.

Put it this way, if camping was really that much fun, rich people would do it. But whenever I see photos of the fabulous and famous on holiday, they're always sipping cocktails in St Tropez. I've never seen footage of Tom and Katie at the Garden of Eden Caravan Park, sitting around an open fire eating a can of Mr Heinz's finest, singing, 'Beans, beans the musical fruit!'

I actually think that's why I don't like camping – because I've been poor. As a uni student and stand-up comedian, I know what it's like to survive for a week on one can of lentils, a packet of two-minute noodles and a cask of wine.

Sure, people argue it's good to be alone with nature. To those I say: Haven't you watched the news lately? Hurricanes, tsunamis, floods and earthquakes. Nature hates us. Being alone with nature is like getting intimate with Ivan Milat.

These same people reckon it's great to get out of the city so you can see the stars. Yeah, but in the city you don't need to see the stars because there are better things to see – like movies, theatre, bands and reasonably priced lap-dancers.

Anyway, despite all my reservations, I did actually go camping a few weeks ago for my friend Mary-Lou's birthday. She's a good mate so I decided the least I could do was try to brave it. And you know what? The experience did actually teach me a couple of things.

For starters, it turns out that when it comes to packing, you can actually be too prepared. By the time I finished shopping, it looked less like I was heading down the coast for a weekend, and more like I was going into a nuclear bunker. I even packed some flares – though I still can't remember why I thought a pair of wide-bottomed jeans would come in handy.

I also invested in a Swiss Army Knife, but after a weekend of using it, I'm convinced Switzerland would be an easy target: 'Get back, or we will use this tiny magnifying glass to slowly burn you.'

The next lesson I learned is, never check out other people's sites. I know the grass is always greener, but some of these people had tents that would have made the Ringley Brothers ashamed. Were they camping or on the run after looting the gift shop on *Sale of the Century*?

Anyway, once you've set up your campsite, don't think it's time to relax, oh no. First you have to collect wood for the fire. Rather than a relaxing weekend, this was like an episode of *Survivor* (where I would have gladly voted myself out).

For those who haven't been camping, it's all about the fire. You use it for heat, cooking and sitting around singing camp songs. (And by that I mean 'Kumbuya', not Kylie's *Greatest Hits* and *The Best of Abba*.)

Because you cook around the fire, every single meal ends up tasting like BBQ. Meat tastes like BBQ, salad tastes like BBQ, breakfast cereal tastes like BBQ and even BBQ shapes taste like BBQ. (In fact, the only thing that doesn't taste like BBQ is human flesh, which still tastes like chicken.)

And not only does the smoke contaminate the food, it also gets into your clothes and hair. By the end of the weekend, I smelt like one of John Elliot's lungs, or as if I'd been making out with Keith Richards.

Of course, my attitude wasn't helped by the lack of sleep. Sure, everyone talks about the peacefulness of nature, but they never tell you about the hundreds of kids who wake you up in the morning doing auditions for *Lord of the Flies*. (Never mind the mosquitoes, the genius who comes up with kiddie-coils is going to make a fortune.)

So, did I have a good time? I have to confess that yes I did, although it did help that with my mates, camping is less an excuse to get back to nature and more a reason to find somewhere new to drink.

Because let's face it, when it comes to alcohol, my thirst is unquenchable. Especially when cocktails are on offer. I can't help it; I get sucked in by all the fancy names promising endless amusement. Every time I enter a bar, I hear the siren song of the cocktail menu luring me towards the rocks with drinks like 'Sex on a Beach' or 'Long Slow Screw Up Against a Wall'.

Of course this never happens. I'm more likely to be at the Rooty Hill RSL, and the best I could hope for is 'Sex in a Ute' or a 'Short Grope Up Against the Pool Table'.

This is obviously a case of misleading advertising. Forget about Telstra or the banks, isn't it time the government pulled Allan Fels out of retirement to investigate cocktail names?

Every other day, the newspaper reports that Australians are drinking too much. Well, there is any easy solution to this. We simply introduce legislation that ensures cocktails are named after what *really* happens when you drink them.

I can guarantee nobody would drink anywhere near as much if they had to order a 'Spew Down My Top'; 'Eat a Hot Chicken Roll from 7-Eleven'; or a row of 'Can't Get it Up' shooters.

But it's not only the names of drinks that suck me in, it's also the ads. I'm a lick, sip, sucker for a good booze ad.

I'm particularly fond of the VB ads. They are just so damned manly, chock-a-block with manly men doing manly things, quite often at the beach (probably Manly).

Big, boofy blokes with their shirts off, chopping wood and fixing cars, saying things like, 'You can get it killing an animal with your bare hands . . . matter of fact I've got it now!'

You never see a VB ad for men like me. A couple of metrosexuals having a drink at a trendy bar saying, 'You can get it watching *Buffy*!'

But not everyone loves alcohol ads as much as I do. There've been calls recently to ban alcohol advertising at sports because some people reckon it sends the wrong message.

(Although if that's the criteria, mobile phone sponsorship should be banned. After all, it's because of mobiles that all sorts of 'wrong' messages have been sent.)

Personally, I don't care either way as long as they make a firm decision. Either ban it all, or make it open slather — now that could be really fun, especially if the booze companies not only sponsored the teams but named them too.

The West Coast Eagles could become the West Coast Coolers; Victoria's cricket team could be known as the Bitters; and don't tell me rugby league wouldn't have more appeal if there was a team called the North Queensland Cock-Sucking Cowboys.

Of course, some people argue it doesn't matter what message the media gives about booze, it's the example you get from home that really matters.

This is particularly true in my case as my father doesn't drink, so all my life I have felt burdened by the pressure to make up for him.

Which is why I'm always the dickhead at the office Christmas party who ends up dancing on the table with his pants around his ankles and a floral lampshade on his head.

Yep, that's right, dear reader. Every year without fail I manage to make a complete arse of myself at the office Christmas party.

Every December I promise myself that this year it's going to be different, but then every year the Christmas spirit enters me – closely followed by the Christmas wine, the Christmas beer, and the Christmas Long Slow Screw Up Against a Wall – and suddenly I'm back on the table looking like Ned Kelly if he'd been visited by Carson from *Queer Eye*.

Of course, the root of the problem can be traced to two simple words: free beer. After 'I love you', 'free' and 'beer' are the best words in the English language. Of course, my favourite sentence of all time is, 'I love you, free beer!'

And if the office Christmas party is about one thing, it's free food and booze. In fact, I even have a formula for calculating just how much I should eat and drink. First, I estimate how much I think I should be getting paid; then I subtract what I actually earn; and the result is how much I have to consume in free grog and nibbles to get even.

(If I feel like I deserve a Christmas bonus, I try to steal some stationery on the way out. Last year I managed a whole photocopier down the front of my pants.)

Unfortunately for my career prospects, booze not only loosens my pants, it has the same effect on my mouth. You know the saying, loose lips sink ships? Well, if my career was the *Titanic*, my tongue would be an iceberg.

I'm the guy who always ruins the party by accidentally insulting my boss's partner. I always intend to say something like, 'Wow, it's nice to meet you, I have heard so much about you' but when processed by Drunkenese, it sounds more like: 'Wow, you're really hot! You're not a hooker, are you?' or 'Were you really drunk when you met him? We all assumed he was gay!'

I'm so good at offending the most important person in the room, I'm thinking of hiring myself out as a freelancer: 'Want to tell your boss he is a big fat prick, but don't have the guts? Hire the W.A. Team. Weddings, parties, anything. Will work for canapés.'

The other thing I excel at is doing something stupid, and getting caught. Put it this way, if you want to photocopy your arse, make sure you don't have any distinguishing moles or tattoos. (And if you're going to photocopy your genitals, set the machine to enlarge. Though you do run the risk of being accused of false advertising if you manage to pick up.)

Anyway, all drunken tomfoolery aside, the trick to behaving yourself at the office Christmas party is to remember that it's actually a business function.

So you didn't grope your client on the dance floor, you 'initiated a merger'; you didn't vomit in the toilet, you 'off-loaded some unnecessary assets'; and you didn't shag Becky from Accounts, you indulged in some 'insider trading'.

(And because it's a business function, if at the end of the night you end up at a lap-dancing club, make sure you get a receipt for every five dollar note you tuck into the stripper's g-string.)

Arguably, the only bash more challenging than the annual Christmas shindig is a fancy-dress party.

The other day I received an invitation and was really excited until I spotted the words that fill me with dread. No, not Bring Your Own Booze. Yep, you guessed it: fancy dress.

Look, I don't want to be a party-pooper, but to me 'fancy dress' is putting on my formal tracksuit pants and a shirt that has less than three stains on it.

While I do concede that fancy-dress parties can certainly have their moments, overall I find them daunting, particularly because I'm forever putting my foot in it.

Put it this way, you should always check that someone is actually in costume before you comment on their outfit: 'Wow, that's an awesome fat Elvis suit . . . oh, sorry . . . yes the buffet is over that way!'

Plus, I have enough trouble recognising people at the best of times, but once I've had a couple of beverages and they are dressed as the Incredible Hulk, it's a lost cause.

'G'day, I'm Wil!'

'Yeah, I know, Wil, it's Gary from Accounts. We speak every day . . . and remember, keep your receipts or you will make me angry, and you're not going to like me when I'm angry!'

For those lucky readers who have never experienced the pleasure of the costume party, there are some things you need to know.

Just like there is always one burnt chip in every packet, and every boy-band has an ugly member, at every fancy-dress party there will always be someone dressed as a Naughty Nurse. (And you get the impression they didn't have to hire the outfit.)

Regardless of the theme, if it's 'animals' they're dressed as the Naughty Grey Nurse Shark, and if it's 'religion' they are the Naughty Nurse that helped deliver Jesus in the manger.

My tip is, try to be just a little bit original. It's bad enough rocking up to a normal party and discovering that someone is wearing the same thing as you, it's even worse when you are both dressed as Spiderman – and their costume is better.

'Ah yes, you are Spiderman. That's cool, I'm Spidey's little-known twin brother Arachnid Boy! I do whatever a spider can too, but in a slightly crappier outfit!'

(And while we're on the topic, if you are going as a superhero, make sure you get a costume that fits. Nobody wants to see Batman become Fatman.)

Beware, though, of putting in too much effort. In other words, if there is a chance you're going to get nominated for best make-up and costume at next year's Oscars, you may want to pull back a little.

This type of party-going perfectionist is forever putting herself down with things like: 'I really don't think this fake blood looks realistic enough!' Yes, because otherwise people might have mistaken you for the real Dracula – well, if we ignore that you are standing in direct sunlight and have just polished off a loaf of garlic bread.

(If you are dressed as a horror character, I would recommend arranging a lift home. You think it's hard hailing a taxi after a few drinks? Try it dressed as Freddy from *Nightmare on Elm Street*. And with those hands, hitching might be a challenge.)

Add to the list of annoying fancy-dressers the couple who always turn up dressed as a classic couple, such as Adam and Eve, Antony and Cleopatra or the Naughty Schoolgirl and the Dodgy PE Teacher.

While the couple idea might seem cute at first, the downside is you have to stand next to each other all night. After all, if you're dressed as Adam and Eve, and Eve is at the bar getting an apple martini then you're just some weird, nude bloke with compost on your serpent.

If you insist on doing the couple thing, at least make it creative: He could go as Michael Jackson when he was a black man, and she could go as Michael Jackson when he was a white woman.

But the worst thing about fancy dress is that it raises too many perplexing questions, such as: If you are asked to a costume party on casual clothes Friday, do you still have to dress up? What does Prince wear if he goes to a fancy-dress party? When Nazis go to costume parties, do they dress up as Prince Harry?

But there are two biggies that need to be answered once and for all: How many times after the party is it acceptable to wear the costume? Because if I've hired it for three days, I want to get my money's worth.

I once hired a native American Indian costume – which I had for a few days – so I'd dress up and go looking for bikers and construction workers, and convince them to join me in a rendition of 'YMCA'.

The final, most important question is: Should you have to Bring Your Own Booze to a fancy-dress party?

Personally, I think not. After all, you've already laid out a fair bit of dosh on your costume; if anything, you should be able to present your receipt at the bar and claim the equivalent amount in free drinks.

Speaking of free drinks, I read the other day that Qantas, Virgin and Jetstar will soon have to compete with a new airline carrier that specialises in parties, pizza nights, karaoke and dance-offs. Or, in other words, pretty much your average flight with Courtney Love.

But while many travellers have greeted this news with excitement, I've got to say I'm sceptical. Don't get me wrong, with the number of times I've been delayed, I reckon the airlines could learn a thing or two from the pizza delivery industry. If it's more than thirty minutes late, it should be free.

But a plane that doubles as a 'Nightclub of the Sky'? I'm not so sure. Imagine presenting your boarding pass to the flight attendant only to be stopped in your tracks by two bouncers: 'Nah, not in those shoes mate.'

But what would freak me out more than anything would be the captain's announcement:

'Ladies and gentlemen, this is your captain peaking. I'm flying, and I hope you are too. If you want to see me taxi down the runway let me hear you say, "Ho"!

'Today we'll be cruising at a height of 30,000 feet, unless of course you've taken one of those lovely purple pills (complimentary in first class) in which case you'll be cruising at a height of 50,000 feet.

'Sorry about the delay in our take-off. I was slightly distracted by a man on the ground waving yellow paddles at me. I'm not quite sure what he was trying to tell me, but man he was going off.

'Earlier, as we taxied along the white take-off line, air traffic control informed me that today's flight-time is estimated to be approximately thirteen hours. Since then, I've taxied along a white line of my own and I reckon I can get us there in about thirty minutes.

'If you care to look out the window right now, you'll notice the people on the ground are so small they appear like ants. Oh my God! They are ants; in fact I'm covered in ants, get them off me!

'At this time may I also remind you to please switch off your mobile phones as we have Shane Warne, David Beckham and Mark Gasnier sitting in first class and it may result in them interfering with their equipment.

'It is now time for our safety demonstration. If you need any assistance during the flight, please push the little button on your armrest, and a small glowing man will appear above your head. For those who've taken the purple pills, this should amuse you for hours.

'Please note that your emergency exits are located here, and here. And if you get lucky in the toilets during the flight, your ankles will be located here and here. (Remember what we say, if the 747's a-rockin' don't come a-knockin'.)

'Speaking of the toilets, please note restrooms on this plane have not been fitted with smoke detectors, but they do have smoke machines to create that authentic night-club feel.

'If cabin lights go out, a series of floorlights will lead you directly to the emergency exit. If these lights fail, please follow the swirling disco ball which will lead you around, and around and around.

'In a moment, we will show you a short movie entitled *Deep Vein Thrombosis* which, despite its promising title, is not a sequel to *Debbie Does Dallas*.

'After this, our in-flight entertainment will feature Bazza and Dazza getting drunk and singing a karaoke version of "I Still Call Australia Home" – which, let's face it, will be a lot more entertaining than the crappy Ben Affleck movies our competitors screen.

'In case of unexpected turbulence, a bong will fall from the roof. This won't help the bumpiness, but it should chill you out. Please breathe deeply yourself before passing it on to your neighbouring passenger.

'In the unlikely event of a crash-landing, please consult the card in the seat pocket in front of you for the emergency brace position. It also shows the macarena, YMCA, bus-stop, time-warp, lambada and mambo No. 5, 6 and 7 for the dance contest later.

'We are about to commence our in-flight meal service. For those who've taken the purple pills, please note the meals are meant to be miniature, the drinks are meant to be miniature, and the cutlery is meant to be miniature. You have not, I repeat, you have not turned into a giant.

'Shortly we will commence our descent, so please return all tray tables to their upright position. And those who've just joined the Mile-High Club, please return the flight attendants to their upright position.

'Please note, your baggage will be available from a carousel on the ground floor. Your emotional baggage should arrive on Tuesday.

'Once again, thank you for flying with Nightclub of the Skies. Others may be cheaper and faster, but we fly the highest.'

One thing's for sure, if I am going to get my kicks thousands of feet above the ground then I'd much rather go skydiving. I did it for the first time recently, and what an exhilarating experience it was. (I should point out that I didn't jump by myself, I did a tandem jump. You see, when it comes to throwing yourself out of a plane, it's the opposite to sex – you start doing it with someone else and when you get good enough they let you do it by yourself.)

So why did I do it? Well, you know that intense feeling of relief you get when you over-balance on a ladder but catch yourself just before you fall? Well, skydiving is like that times a million. Forget taking drugs such as E, GBH or LSD, the best rush you can ever get is AD: Almost Dying.

So the place where I scored my AD was Tyagarah airfield, courtesy of the good people at Skydive Byron Bay. But first I had to fill in some forms. So many forms, in fact, I was starting to think that perhaps the jump should be a three-way tandem: me, my instructor, and my lawyer.

My favourite part was the warning down the bottom: 'Skydiving is Dangerous'. Well duh, thanks for that. To be fair, my instructors were very conscious of safety, right up to the massive 'No Smoking' sign on the wall of the hangar. Yeah, that's a good point. When you're about to jump out of a plane, you don't want to be exposed to something hazardous like passive smoking.

Anyway, forms filled, each of the first-time free-fallers was assigned a Tandem Master (which sounds like something from Dungeons and Dragons).

Nathan (my tandem master) was a top bloke, and I quickly asked him if he had plans for that night. I just wanted to make sure he had something worth living for.

Then we started getting dressed. Firstly, they gave me a pair of parachute pants, which despite going out of fashion around the time of MC Hammer, I wore anyway. (I suspect they serve the purpose of protecting your instructor from the 'fear' running down the inside of your leg.)

Then came the strapping-in of the safety gear, which made me look less like I was about to jump out of a plane and more like I was going to the Hellfire Club. I'm convinced the kid who first came up with the wedgie at primary school went on to a fine career designing parachute equipment.

Then before you could say, 'Oh my God! This is scarier than Gretel Killeen's fashion sense!' we were being loaded onto the plane. (Or as the instructors call it: 'The point of no refund'.) There were about ten of us crammed in and strapped to the floor. Sure it was cramped, wet and cold, but still more luxurious than Jetstar. (We were so close that when we hit an air-pocket, Nathan and I accidentally joined the Mile-high Club.)

As the plane circled higher, the tandem masters started letting loose with the black humour. There was a lot of, 'Wow, I am really hung-over this morning'; and 'Oh, I thought we got this clip fixed'. My girlfriend Amy was referred to as my 'Next of Kin'; and someone even dusted off the old classic: 'Why don't blind people skydive? Because it scares the hell out of the dog!'

Then suddenly we were at 14,000 feet; the moment of truth. First out of the plane was Stace, our camera person, who I'd hired so I had a memento of the occasion – or in the worst-case scenario, Amy would at least be able to win the 5000 bucks on *Funniest Home Videos*.

And then one, two, three, oh my God! and we were freefalling. 10,000 feet at over 230 kmph. Pure AD.

Once I'd opened my eyes and checked my dacks, I noticed that the minute you jump out of a plane, everyone turns into Keanu Reeves. The only words you can say are 'awesome', 'wicked', and 'woooooo!' I guess it'd be rare for someone to be freefalling at 230 kmph and say, 'So, what do you think about the leadership tensions in the Liberal Party?'

The second thing is, no one in the world can skydive and look good at the same time. With your eyes bulging and your skin flapping wildly, you end up with a remarkable resemblance to John Laws. (Don't even get me started on my hair, which looked like something even Thorpie would have frowned at.)

And then before I knew it, the chute was open, and I was floating peacefully back to earth. Apparently Nathan and I had a bad landing – although in my opinion, any landing you can walk away from cannot be bad.

But if you really want to scare yourself shitless, then hire out *Wolf Creek*. Holy, moley, that movie is scary. Think Rose Hancock without her make-up, or Amanda Vanstone doing an impression of Jessica Simpson in the film-clip for *These Boots Are Made for Walking*. Yep, it's that terrifying.

Rather than there not being a dry eye in the house, in this movie there wasn't a dry seat. It's rated R, as in: 'Argghh, lucky I got this jumbo popcorn, I think I might need the bucket.'

Quentin Tarantino called it the scariest film he'd ever seen, which is like Shannon Noll criticising a singer for being a bit nasal, or Shane Warne calling someone a root-rat.

Put it this way, if they ever screen it on TV, they'll have to start half an hour earlier just to play the pre-film warnings. (Although if they edit the violence, some of the ads will run longer than the film.)

It's so gut-wrenching, people have walked out of screenings. (Although this is not completely unusual for an Australian film. At the premiere of *Crocodile Dundee in LA*, even the cast walked out.)

But if you can stomach it, *Wolf Creek* is a brilliant movie. In fact, it's the best Australian film I've seen since *Mad Max*. (Admittedly, though, I'm the sort of film-goer who reckons *Lantana* would've been better if a violent psycho had killed half the cast with a chainsaw.)

Now I don't want to get all Margaret Pomeranz on yo asses, but not only does *Wolf Creek* tell a gripping tale, feature some great acting and excellent direction, the cinematography is beautiful. That is, the pictures look rooly, rooly good. I was stunned to discover that the film was originally shot on high-definition, which is like finding out that *Schindler's List* was shot on Steven

Spielberg's mobile phone, or the Mona Lisa was scribbled on the back of a cocktail napkin.

Of course, *Wolf Creek* hasn't been without controversy. For starters, some in the tourism industry reckon its storyline might discourage backpackers from visiting Australia.

I've got only one thing to say about that. Good. In fact, I wish they'd set the film in Bondi. The villain, Mick Taylor, could have 'evicted with extreme prejudice' the twenty or so whingeing Poms who are permanently packed into every two-bedroom flat.

Here's an idea: Let's not condemn Mick, let's recruit him. He could be our secret weapon in getting back the Ashes. Let's see how Andrew Flintoff reacts when Australia's opening bowling attack is Glenn McGrath and Mick Taylor.

But all joking aside, it's just a movie, is it really going to stop people coming here? Did people stop buying used cars after seeing *Christine*? Post *Psycho* did people put an end to showers? Come on, tourism in New Zealand actually went up after *Lord of the Rings*. Nobody stayed at home because they were terrified of being eaten by Orcs.

Wolf Creek is an absolute cracker, but by far the best thing about the movie is John Jarratt's performance as Mick. This bloke makes Hannibal Lector seem like Nelson Mandela.

Jarratt gives the performance of his life (yep, even better than *McLeod's Daughters*) and the fact that he didn't get nominated for Best Actor at the AFIs is an absolute disgrace. I suspect they were afraid to entrust such a sharp and pointy object to someone that terrifying.

Speaking of which, I was lucky enough to scam an invite to the recent AFI Awards – I told them I played the creek in *Wolf Creek* – and in case you didn't catch it on telly (which wouldn't surprise me, given that it was screened at the prime time of 11 o'clock on a Saturday night) here's a brief report.

The award ceremony was hosted by Russell Crowe, who I have to say did a pretty good job keeping the whole shebang shebanging. (Although he could've saved some time by throwing the awards at the winners.)

Sure, some party-poopers have argued that on a night celebrating Australian film and TV, he shouldn't have sung a song at the end, but I thought it was a great idea. It's often quite a challenge to clear a crowd after a big awards night, but Rusty took care of it.

In case you missed it, Russell finished the show by doing a duet with Marcia Hines. (A bit of advice, Russ: When you don't have the best voice in the world, don't do a duet with someone who does. Put it this way, there's a reason Renae Lawrence never stands next to Michelle Leslie.)

Oh, and did you hear the good news? Russ has a new band. Thirty Odd Foot of Grunt is no more, and has been replaced with Russell Crowe and The Ordinary Fear of God.

It sounds less like a band-name and more like the title of a Booker Prize-winning novel. I can't imagine what his next band will be: Russell Crowe and the Life of Pi? The Unbearable Lightness of Being Russell Crowe? The Russ Whisperer?

Have you noticed the names have something in common?

Thirty Odd Foot of Grunt and The Ordinary Fear of God both have the acronym TOFOG.

Do you reckon Rusty had some old TOFOG merchandise hanging around that he didn't want to waste? What's his next band going to be called, Ten Obese Flatulent Old Geezers?

But I digress: Apart from the fine work of Russ Crowe, I do have one personal highlight from the AFIs.

Now I don't want to blow my own trumpet – I tried once, nearly put my back out – but *The Glass House* did win an AFI Award for Best Light Entertainment.

This came as a massive shock because I've become so accustomed to losing to Andrew Denton that I thought my gravestone would read: 'It was nice to be nominated.'

It was also a major surprise because Hughesy, Corinne and I were sitting so far from the stage, I reckon we were in a different suburb. I assumed we didn't have a chance given we'd have to take public transport to get to the podium.

Anyway, I finally made it up there and delivered a rather embarrassing acceptance speech, due no doubt, to the few quiet shandies I had at the ABC pre-ceremony drinks. (Okay, if I'm honest, I tried to make up for the raise I didn't get by drinking the equivalent amount in free champagne; I may have even drunk my way into a new tax bracket.)

Standing up on stage making a fool of myself actually comes rather naturally to me. I was reminded of performing at the recent Comedy Festival in Melbourne; that time of year when an Australian comedian, an English comedian and an Irish comedian walk into a pub – and don't come out for another month.

While performing at the festival is certainly the most fun I can have with 400 strangers but missing a giant tub of jelly, hydraulic equipment and Paris Hilton, it is also really hard work.

Not that I want to complain. After all, despite what some people would have you believe, stand-up comedy is not the toughest job the world. Where else could you turn up for one hour a day, spend most of that time drinking and talking about yourself, and at the end be applauded instead of sacked?

That said, it can be unforgiving when you first start; there is no Humourversity or School of Hard Knock-Knocks where you can enrol in Comedy 101.

The really terrifying thing is that on your first day of work, you're expected to perform the exact same job as the most experienced players: stand before a room of strangers and try to make them laugh. Let's face it, at most jobs they don't even entrust you with the photocopier on your first day.

That's why festivals are so important. It's a wonderful time for performers to get together and learn from and inspire each other. (Okay, and shag, bitch about and steal from each other.)

But the festival also brings some worries. Firstly, you are constantly anxious that no one will turn up to your show. While most comedians would probably perform regardless – there's only a fine line and a cardboard box that separates most comics from that crazy guy on the street – an audience certainly helps. At the very least, you get a pretty good idea how you're going.

Then there's the critics. One of the creative challenges of any festival is transforming a review that reads, 'This show was the greatest waste of time. It made me regret every single minute of my life. I wish I was dead. The only thing funny was the smell on my clothes after. He is a talentless wanker. No star', into a poster quote that reads, 'This show was the greatest . . . every single minute . . . was dead . . . funny. He is a . . . star.'

And of course let's not forget the hecklers. Personally, I don't mind them; that is, if I can understand what they are saying. I was once heckled by a Scottish guy with a brogue so thick I needed subtitles. It was like being heckled by SBS.

I found out later he'd said, 'Australians are so lazy, you wouldn't pull a greasy stick out of a dog's bum!' What? I'd never heard that before. I'd certainly never seen it on *Burgo's Catch Phrase*.

But even when you can make out what they're shouting, dealing with hecklers isn't usually a problem. After all, most punters didn't pay 35 bucks to listen to a drunk idiot dribble crap. (Er . . . come to think of it, that's a pretty accurate description of my show. In fact, I think it's the blurb we used in the program.)

But every joker knows by heart the sobering tale of the comic who, despite completing twenty minutes of his routine, still hadn't managed to get a laugh. As the crickets started to heckle and so many tumbleweeds rolled across the stage, the comic played his final, desperate card – audience participation.

Spotting an old bloke in the audience, he asked him his name. The man looked back at him, slightly surprised, and in a softly spoken Irish brogue answered, 'Dave Allen'.

Suddenly all the oxygen was sucked out of the room as the audience held its breath. But the worst was still to come. Not recognising one of Ireland's most famous comedians, the young joker pursued his line of questioning. 'So Dave,' he continued, 'what do you do?'

Allen looked back at the young lad, paused and then quietly replied, 'I'm a comedian. What do you do?'

As well as the Comedy Festival, my other favourite annual gathering is the Big Day Out. Where else can you see over fifty bands in one place for 110 bucks? Do the math: that's just over two bucks a band, or about the same as you'd pay for Daryl Somers' new album.

As a keen music lover, I've been lucky enough to attend over thirty Big Day Outs (or is it Big Days Out like Grands Prix?). I hope to have a few more left in me before I start resembling Iggy Pop.

While I have great memories of some, and no memories of the other, even better ones, I've come to realise that what I really love about the Big Day Out happens off-stage. Yes, my friends, to quote *The Castle*, it's all about the vibe.

Sure, I love seeing the best bands in the world, but I get just as much joy from watching someone who has forked out $120 of their hard-earned cash trying to ride a wheelie bin as if it's a rodeo bull.

The real joy of the festival for me is that it brings people together. It's the only place you'll see a Cronulla surfer standing next to a

Lebanese Muslim standing next to a fifty-year-old man dressed as a schoolgirl – all united by their love of music. One of my favourite sights is the teenager with jeans so low people are using his crack to park their bikes, standing next to Dad who reckons he's cool but if he wore his belt any higher he'd be Michael Hutchence.

I guess you could say the Big Day Out is like a uniting of the tribes, except that instead of traditional native American names like Dances With Wolves, the kids would be called things like Dances to Doof, Spews Down His Shirt, and Gropes in the Port-a-loo.

And how do you identify the tribes? Well, by their outfits, of course. From the White Stripes fans dressed in black, white and red (resembling the St Kilda cheer squad), to bogan blokes with watermelons on their heads who look like they've been dressed by Beer Eye for the Straight Guy.

Then there's the skinny, young girls dressed in nothing but tiny shorts and bikinis (where do they keep their money?) and the young shirtless blokes with slogans in zinc cream all over their bodies. (Do they realise that after a long day in the sun, they'll have a tan on their forehead that reads, 'Yay, for boobies!'

And let's not forget the punks and metal-heads with so many piercings, you could play an entire round of mini-golf using only the holes in their bodies.

Or the blue-haired punk-lite kids who can't afford hair dye so by the end of the gig, their faces are covered with food colouring. You can't tell if they are punks or Smurfs.

And then there's one of my faves: the girls in stilettos who are now stuck in the mud, ducking the loose change people are tossing at them because they've been mistaken for busking statues.

But without a doubt my absolute favourites are the Goths who, regardless of the weather, always come dressed head to toe in black, often vinyl, and thick make-up. No wonder they seem permanently depressed. By the end of a forty-degree summer day, it's like a scene from *The Wizard of Oz*: 'I'm melting, I'm melting!'

All these different people, united by their love of music; it really is an amazing day. Well, apart from one little, tiny, teeny weeny thing – the port-a-loos. I'm sorry, but by the end of a hot summer's day, those stink boxes emit odours that are banned under the Geneva Convention.

Every year my thighs ache for days after, not from the dancing, moshing or rushing from stage-to-stage, but from trying to hover above the port-a-loo toilet so my bum doesn't touch the seat.

So what's the solution? Well, I always remember to pack a texta, a sheet of paper and some blank sticky-tape. Then I make sure I get to the grounds early, find a nice clean toilet, and hang a sign on the door that says: 'Out of Order'. Voilà, you have your own private executive washroom.

Oh yes, I am the MacGyver of music festivals. See you in the mosh-pit.

SIX

LIFESTYLES OF THE RICH AND DUMB

Did you know that the Wiggles are Australia's highest paid entertainers? According to a recent *BRW* Rich List, they earned more than $45 million in 2004 – or as I refer to it, about $44,950,000 MTM (More Than Me).

Not bad for a group who resemble life-size fluorescent novelty condoms and whose trademark is to imitate an AFL goal umpire with Parkinson's disease. (They now have a legitimate use for that weird finger motion: counting their huge wads of cash.)

Yep, the Big Red Car is about to become the Big Gold Car, with mags, spoilers and sub-woofers pumping out 'Cold Spaghetti' in stereophonic surround-sound.

While the Wiggles certainly deserve their success, as an entertainer myself, I have to admit that looking over this *BRW* list of the Fifty Richest Entertainers was a bit disheartening. I mean, you always expect to earn less than Russell Crowe and Nicole Kidman, but it's a bit pathetic when you get your butt kicked by Captain Feathersword and Dorothy the Dinosaur. Clearly, things aren't going too well when you're still renting, but Wags the Dog has just bought his own place.

The Wiggles actually knocked Nicole Kidman from the top of the list, although she still had a pretty decent harvest, raking in $40 million ($39, 950,000 MTM). Not bad when you consider it included *The Stepford Wives*, a movie so bad that by the time I got out of the cinema, they'd already taken down the sign, sold all the posters, and released it on DVD.

I have to say, though, that despite featuring in what was arguably the year's most-hyped but worst movie, I don't begrudge Nicole any of her fortune. You see, Nicole and I are *like this*. I've even been on a date with her. Okaay, you've twisted my arm. I'll digress and tell you about it.

A few years ago on Tripe J, Adam Spencer and I interviewed the lovely Ms Kidman, and asked her to comment on the rumours about her love-life. (At the time, the gossip mags had her dating everyone from Jude Law to her fake nose from *The Hours*.)

She laughed and said the problem was, every time she was seen with a man, the media assumed they were having hot, steamy sex. Which prompted one of my better ideas: 'Well, next time you're in the country,' I said, 'why don't you have a drink with me; it would be awesome for my reputation!'

That was the moment Nicole Kidman learned the Paris Hilton

lesson – it's all well and good to have fun, but just don't do it on tape – because she replied, 'Okay, I'm back at Christmas, let's go for a drink then!'

We must have played that audio grab about a thousand times, to the point where even the guy who programs *The Simpsons* thought we were overdoing it. A piece of tape hasn't been stretched that thin since Sharon Stone's leg-crossing scene in *Basic Instinct* came out on VCR. By Christmas, the recording was so warped it was hard to tell if it was Nicole Kidman agreeing to have a drink with me, or Peter Harvey . . . Canberra.

Sadly though, Christmas came and the promised drink never eventuated. So in the New Year, when I spotted a picture of Nicole visiting sick children at a Sydney hospital, I thought I'd take matters into my own hands.

Launching into my best John Laws, I started pounding the table: 'How dare you, Nicole? How dare you be seen with sick children when you are meant to be having a drink with me? It makes me sick! I don't care if they are make-a-wish kids, how about my wish to pash you?'

And that's when the studio phone started ringing. Now normally, if Adam Spencer handed me a phone and said, 'It's Nicole Kidman on the line', I'd think he was joking, but he said it in that voice you reserve for statements like, 'Both your parents are dead.'

It was indeed Ms Kidman, who was such a good sport, she not only agreed to have a drink with me, but also allowed us to do a talkback segment on where we might go. (My fave was the listener who suggested Moonlight Cinema to see *Mission Impossible*.)

In the end, we agreed to meet at my local RSL, and to my absolute surprise, just like my teenage sex life, she came alone. No publicists, no managers, no bodyguards or nipple-tweakers, just a down-to-earth, smart, friendly, and surprisingly funny Aussie chick having a few 1970s price beers at the local rissole.

(Although I must say for the record, we had three rounds and I got all three. They obviously didn't have change for a million-dollar note at the RSL.)

Which reminds me: I should get back to the *BRW* rich list. After Nicole, Russell Crowe came next with $27 million (or $26,950,000 MTM) but remember, that has to keep him in flannelette shirts and angry pills for an entire year. (Seriously, does Russ own a change of clothes? All I've ever seen him wear is a pair of jeans, a T-shirt and a bulldog-emblazoned bomber jacket.)

And with all that spare cash floating around, he'd do well to buy himself a mobile phone. For $100 he could get one for himself and a freebie for Danielle. That way he might avoid the bother of ripping hotel phones out of walls – as you do – and asking reception why they don't work. ('Because it's not plugged in, you idiot!') It's no wonder *Cinderella Man* dogged. Why pay good money when you can see Rusty punching people in the face for free?

Personally, I think Hollywood keeps miscasting him. Instead of *A Beautiful Mind* or *Master and Commander*, they should've cast him as the Incredible Hulk. Or perhaps he is simply taking the *Cinderella Man* theme too far; every time he stays out after midnight, his head turns into a pumpkin. (You know how in big hotels they often have codenames for celebrities? They have a new one for Russell; it's 'Duck!'.

Russell may have made it even higher up the rich list if he'd pursued a different career path. It's a little-known fact, but like the Wiggles, Rusty once considered working as a children's entertainer. Problem is, he kept copping flak for giving the kids Chinese burns when they wouldn't let him finish his poems.

There are also rumours that Russell is currently negotiating the movie rights to the big-screen version of the Wiggles' 'Hot Potato, Hot Potato', but only if he gets full script approval and can play the part of the Potato.

If you wanted to be a rich entertainer in 2004, acting seemed a good career choice. There were fourteen actors on the *BRW* list – well, thirteen plus Heath Ledger.

I have to admit, I've never understood the whole Heath Ledger fascination. After seeing most of his movies, I'd like to describe his performances as wooden, but that would be unfair to trees. (He was so bad in *A Knight's Tale*, a family of squirrels tried to store their nuts in him.) At times, he is even out-acted by the scenery. He makes Keanu Reeves seem as animated as Robin Williams. Even Cher has more emotion in her face – and she's made entirely from Tupperware.

Off the top of my head, I can't think of one good movie he has ever made. He's an entertainment vampire; he sucks the life out of film. If he was inadvertently captured in your holiday snapshots, he'd ruin them. Paris Hilton should've had sex with him in that video; nobody would have seen it. The only person who has more straight-to-video releases is Osama Bin Laden.

Plus, he seems to be nothing but a grumpy, spoiled brat who doesn't respect interviewers or even his fellow actors. In fact, he recently said that actors who do multimillion dollar ad campaigns are whores. (As opposed to actors who do multimillion dollar blockbuster movies: they are high-class escorts.)

In his defence, Heath has said he doesn't care about his image, which would at least explain some of his clothing choices. I'm no fashion expert – I always thought Calvin Klein was the bloke who owned my undies before me – but Heath invariably looks like he's taken a bath in glue. Did he get a makeover from Blind Eye for the Straight Guy?

I understand that he doesn't want to talk to the press about his private life, fair enough. (Although if you really want to keep it private, here's a tip Heath: Stop dating famous people. First there was Heather Graham, then Naomi Watts and now Michelle Williams. Do you get the *FHM 100 Hottest Women* and use it like a home-shopping catalogue?)

What I don't get is his reticence to do publicity for his films. Surely if you're proud of something, you'd want everyone to see it? And in order to do that, you might have to give a lot of interviews. Well, boo-bloody-hoo, call someone who cares. (Maybe Russell Crowe can throw you a phone.)

It's part of your job, and in the real world we all have aspects of our work that suck. If you really hate it that much, here's a visualisation you might want to use. The next time an interviewer asks you about your new movie, your glamorous lifestyle, or the beautiful women you've dated, close your eyes and . . . think about getting a real job.

So anyway, back to the list. It was a good year for Naomi Watts – and not only because she got rid of Heath Ledger. Watts made $17 million ($16,950,000 MTM), which explains why she did *The Ring Two*. And will probably do *The Ring 3*, and *The Ring 4, 5, 6, 7*, and *The Ring 8: Mission to Moscow*. By the time she finishes, she'll have more rings than the opening ceremony of the Nude Olympics.

It was a good year for the Blanchett family, with Cate coming seventh at $13 million, while her husband scored first place on the list of Luckiest Blokes in the Entire Universe.

When I think glamour, she's the only name that springs to mind. Cate takes my breath away. Every time I see her, I sound like Darth Vader trying to run up stairs.

Okay, here's how much I love Mrs Upton: She actually makes me want to go and see Australian films, something I swore I would never do after I saw *You and Your Stupid Mate*. (Did you hear they are using Australian films to interrogate suspects at Guantanamo Bay?)

But for Cate, I went to see *Little Fish*, which to my disappointment wasn't the sequel to *Finding Nemo*, but was excellent nevertheless.

(Although to be honest, I probably would've thought *You and Your Stupid Mate* was excellent if Cate had played the part of 'You' or his 'Stupid Mate'.)

And that's another thing about Cate Blanchett. Not only is she glamorous and beautiful, she's won so many awards she can use them to play a game of Acting Award chess.

Another one of her attributes is that despite her success, she hasn't let fame go to her head; like after the Oscars when a reporter asked her if she was going to change. In one of the most Aussie moments of the year she shot back, 'Absolutely, asshole. You better believe it.'

She is incredibly self-deprecating, especially when she explains her choice of certain roles. She once said she accepted the role of the elf Queen in *Lord of the Rings* because she'd always wanted to appear in a movie wearing big pointy ears. (Well, it was either that or play Tony in the Tony Abbott Story.)

But in the end, it's not her glamorous looks or brilliant acting that I adore the most about Cate Blanchett: It's her choice in men. Yep, that's right, I'm talking about her hubby Andrew Upton, award-winning playwright, and as I said earlier, current holder of the Luckiest Bloke in the Entire Universe title.

Now I don't mean any disrespect to Andy, but remember the euphemism people use when they set you up on a blind date? 'They've got a great personality and an excellent sense of humour.' Well, Andrew must be Robin Williams and Billy Connolly rolled into one.

I'm not trying to be mean; I think it's great that Cate has looked beyond the chocolate on the outside of the Kinder Surprise and found the toy inside. And I hope they are forever happy together.

But if things don't work out, I would love it if Cate would consider me, because while it might not seem like it, when you examine the evidence, Cate and I have a lot in common.

For example, Cate was included in US *People* magazine's Fifty

Most Beautiful People. I sent my nude photo to Australian *People*'s Home Blokes section. I know, it's almost spooky, isn't it? But wait, there's more.

When Cate was filming *The Missing* with Tommy Lee Jones, she went to Cowboy Camp. When I went to Oxford Street the other night, I met a very camp cowboy. She was also in the movie *Paradise Road*, and my favourite song is 'Paradise City' by Guns N' Roses. Coincidence? I think not.

And finally, Cate was beaten for an Oscar by Gwyneth Paltrow, whereas I was beaten for a Logie by *Kath and Kim* (and *The Chaser*, and Andrew Denton, and I think one year by *Backyard Blitz*).

Speaking of backyards, I'm beginning to suspect that Don Burke might be cultivating a special stash in Burke's Attic under Burke's Hydroponic Equipment because – to get back to our list – he lobbed in at number twelve, with $7.2 million.

Television, generally, seems quite lucrative. Rove had another good year, making $5.5 million; although most of that was due to the sale of his Gold Logies – one to John Wood and the other to Kerry-Anne Kennerley.

Eddie McGuire came in at number thirty, with $3.5 million. Which is no great revelation because just as you can tell the age of a tree by the amount of rings it has, Eddie's millions can be measured by counting his double chins. And let's not forget the size of his head. When he was recently head-hunted to be the big-wig at Channel Nine, he was easy enough to locate: Apparently, along with the Great Wall of China, Eddie's head is the only thing you can see from outer space.

All power to him, I say; I reckon he'll do a great job. In fact, the only downside is that station meetings might take a hell of a lot longer: 'Have you been sacked, demoted, still have a job, or given a raise . . .? We'll be back after the break to find out!'

But it does raise the million-dollar question: Just how many gigs can one guy get? No wonder there are still people who can't find work in this country; Eddie has all the freaking jobs.

Yep, it turns out the government didn't need to rush through new IR laws; they should've simply assassinated Eddie. One thing's for sure: Eddie is now one of Australia's most powerful people. Some commentators have even suggested that the Channel Nine gig is a mere stepping-stone on Eddie's journey to the Lodge. (Although why he'd take the massive pay-cut is beyond me.)

Personally, I think he's aiming even higher. Forget the prime ministership, Eddie has his sights set on the Vatican, with his first announcement bound to be proclaiming Nathan Buckley as a saint. (And I don't mean trade him to St Kilda.) Then it would be time to start lobbying for the boss's job. 'Our Father who art in Heaven, Eddie be thy Name!'

Given our society's obsession with fame and wealth, it's no wonder *Who Wants to Be a Millionaire?* is such a popular show. To everyone's great relief, someone actually won the million bucks (a) thank God (b) it's about time (c) congratulations or (d) who gives a crap, I watch *Desperate Housewives*?

Personally, I got pretty excited for Australia's newest millionaire, Rob Fulton, if only because for a while it seemed the only person who was ever going to make a million bucks was Eddie McGuire.

And while to Kerry Packer it may be the loose change that falls down the back of his couch, to most people a million bucks is a mountain of moula. I mean, just think what you could do with a million dollars. You could almost buy an entire tank of petrol.

But joking aside, it's a good thing the major prize finally went off. We were reaching the point where the show's only source of excitement was noting whether Eddie McGuire could pronounce any of the l's in millionaire. (He is probably the only bloke in Australia who can pronounce Sol Trujillo's name.)

And it's been a long time coming. Here's an amazing stat: Since the show started, there've been more than 3 million calls to the show's player registration line. (Although many of them were from confused teenagers who were trying to vote Eddie off the show.)

No doubt about it, it's an amazing story. Rob Fulton went from having twenty bucks in his wallet to one million dollars. He now says he wants to have a crack at *Temptation*. Although if I won a million bucks, I'd want to have a crack at Lavinia Nixon.

I'm just relieved he didn't say he was going to spend the money on the mortgage or sending the kids to a better school like most contestants do. Sure, that's really noble and all, but for once I'd love someone to say, 'Well, Eddie, if I win the money I'm going to spend it all on beer and strippers.'

(And if anybody ever says the words, 'I'll still go to work tomorrow' after a big win, Eddie should take the money back after punching them in the face.)

I have to admit, I quite like *Millionaire*, but I've always thought the first two lifelines are a bit of a waste. For starters, 50/50 always seems to eliminate the two answers you already knew weren't right. 'Okay, so we now know that the President of Uruguay isn't (a) a shoe or (c) the bloke who used to play Urkel on *Family Matters*.'

And then there's Ask the Audience. I'll tell you what I would ask: 'Just how empty is your life that you want to sit in the audience of a live taping of *Who Wants to Be a Millionaire?* At least go to *Deal or No Deal* where you might get to carry a briefcase, or *The Price is Right* where you may even get to 'come on down'.

My favourite of the lifelines is the Phone-a-Friend. They recommend that when you choose your Phone-a-Friend, nominate the first four people in your speed-dial at home. But that wouldn't really work for me unless the question was, 'What are the ingredients of a large vegetarian pizza?'

Personally, I'd forget about my dumb mates and just dial Information; either that or do what most contestants seem to these days, and call a mate who has broadband and is a wizard at Google.

(I love the way they pretend to be thinking of the answer while frantic typing is going on in the background. 'Oh no, we're not looking on the Net, Eddie. That's just our one thousand monkeys compiling the complete works of Shakespeare.')

But though I do like the show, I think together with a new host, they should bring in some changes, just to make it a little bit more exciting.

For starters, how about just occasionally making the correct answer (e) none of the above?

Or instead of writing out a boring cheque, what if they coated the contestants in glue, let them roll around in the cash and keep whatever sticks to them? Or better still, just give them Eddie's ATM card and PIN number?

And to update the Phone-a-Friend option, how about Phone-a-Stranger? You just dial a random number and see what happens.

Or even better, Phone-an-Enemy, where contestants have to ring someone who really hates them, and then decide whether their answer is trustworthy.

And I would like to see more theme shows, like one where all the questions come from songs: 'For $32,000, how deep is your love? For $64,000, how do you mend a broken heart? And for $125,000, do you know the way to San Jose?'

Or perhaps a philosophy edition: 'If a tree falls in the forest and no-one hears it, does it make a sound?' Or a rhetorical question edition where the questions are asked, but no one expects an answer?

Or how about a comedy edition where the questions are based on famous jokes: 'Why did the chicken cross the road?'; 'Knock knock, who's there?'; and 'How many roadies does it take to change a light bulb? Is it (a) one (b) two or (c) one two, one two.'

One thing I hope they *don't* do is drag onto the show a bunch of piss-weak celebrities. (I admit I did love watching Warnie on *Celebrity Millionaire*, despite being disappointed that he didn't ask his Phone-a-Friend, 'So, what are you wearing?')

From *Dancing with the Stars*, *Australia's Brainiest* and *Celebrity Circus* to *Skating on Thin Ice*, *Friday Night Games* and *Celebrity Overhaul*, every night I turn on the news, I half-expect it to be hosted by Leo Sayer. (With Rikki Lee doing the weather.)

The most spectacular success in the celebrity stakes is the number one show, *Dancing with the Stars*. This is an amazing achievement. *Dancing* winning the ratings with Dags as host is like Makybe Diva winning the Melbourne Cup with Kim Beazley as the jockey.

Okay, I have to confess I don't mind *Dancing* – it's like a car crash, you know you shouldn't look but you can't help it – but I do think it'd be better if instead of the tango and the mambo, the contestants had to perform night-club dancing.

Imagine Kostya Tzu belting out the nutbush, or Grant Denyar doing the pelvic thrust in the Time Warp? And what about Jennifer Hawkins and Kate Langbroek dancing around their handbags while the blokes stand aside and drink VB?

(I also have an idea for a much more entertaining show. It's called *Smuggling with the Stars* and it features various celebs trying to smuggle drugs into Bali. The sequel could be *Celebrity Executions*.)

Then there's the ironically named *Australia's Brainiest* franchise, because anyone with half a brain would refuse to appear on the show. They should rename it *Australia's Most Desperate for Publicity*.

But in TV-land, if you have a dead horse there's only one thing to do – flog it. So far we've seen *Australia's Brainiest Comedian*, *Australia's Brainiest Radio Hosts Who Happen to Be Comedians*, and who could forget *Australia's Brainiest TV Presenter Who is Also a Radio Host and a Comedian*.

What's that sound? The bottom of a barrel being scraped? Not even close. Then they showed *Australia's Brainiest Olympian, Musician* and *Big Brother Housemate*. What's next: *Australia's Brainiest Rugby League Player*? And the specialist category tonight is 'spelling your own name'!

Why stop there? Why not *Australia's Brainiest Brain Surgeon*? Or *Australia's Brainiest Guy Who Washes the Windows at the Traffic Lights*? Or 'Tonight Chopper Read, Ivan Milat and various members of the Melbourne underworld on *Australia's Brainiest Mass Murderer*!'

It seems punters will peruse any piece of poo as long as it features a game-show host or former footballer. We even had the *Celebrity Poker Challenge*, although there is no truth to the rumour that this is also the title of Paris Hilton's latest video.

Sadly, the celebs didn't play with their own money, so we didn't get to see Tom Williams lose his shirt, or Jeff having to explain to the other Wiggles why Georgie Parker now owns the Big Red Car.

I think the real appeal of these shows is that average punters enjoy watching celebrities make dicks of themselves. Which explains, I guess, the popularity of the gossip mags.

I picked one up the other day and couldn't believe the foolishness. Top-of-the-pops has got to be Ms Oops I Did it Again, Britney Spears.

Did you hear that she got married for the second time recently? Wow, she must really love wedding cake. At this rate she'll soon overtake that other class-act, J-Lo. Perhaps that's Britney's aim, because I heard at her last wedding, she threw the bouquet and then ran to catch it herself. Or perhaps she just wants to get her money's worth on her wedding frock.

But while I wish the happy Springer-Episode-in-Waiting couple well, surely getting married twice in one year is a bit extreme?

Basically, you know you're getting hitched too often when your wedding finger has more rings than the Olympic flag; the marriage certificate reads 'To whom it may concern'; and during the vows the priest asks, 'Do you, Britney, take Insert Name Here?'

(Of course, it's doubtful that Britney said 'I do' herself; she would've mimed it to a pre-recording.)

But perhaps getting hitched is just an excuse to attract more publicity because, let's face it, celebrity weddings are big business these days, and they sure pull in the punters.

Remember when Mary Donaldson married the Crown Prince of Denmark? Despite it screening in a time-slot usually allocated for infomercials and televangelists, the live coverage of the nuptials attracted over one million viewers. (And the replay on Channel Seven reached an audience of 880,000.)

But the question remains, apart from the assertion that it's every girl's (and about 10 per cent of boys') dream to be a princess, why did Australians get so excited about this wedding?

For starters, I think it's because the happy couple seem to be so down to earth. Plus, ever since Our Tom left Our Nicole, the job of Australia's Favourite Son-in-Law has been wide open – and who better to fill it than a bloke named Fred. Most Aussies love the idea of a royal couple called Fred and Mary; it's only one small step removed from Prince Darren and Princess Sharon.

The fairytale of how Freddy met Mary is also an inspiration to any girl who's dreamed of meeting their prince in a bar. Only this time, the tale didn't go sour the next morning because Mary didn't wake up next to a frog.

My favourite moment of the wedding had to be Mary's kilt-wearing dad doing his best Sharon Stone impression in front of Queen Margrethe as he sat with his legs akimbo for the duration of the ceremony. This continues that long Australian tradition of Dad embarrassing everyone by flashing his nuts at family occasions.

At least he didn't follow that other great Aussie tradition of getting pissed and delivering a speech chock-full of insults and obscenities. I'm not sure how the world's royals would've reacted to him reading a telegram from Mr and Mrs Farkin and the whole Farkin family; or expressing his hope that their honeymoon was like the Nullarbor Plain, one long route.

About the only thing that disappointed me about the wedding was Australia's gift to the happy couple. While Fred and Mez were receiving cars, yachts and a $2.7 million dinner set from the rest of the world, the Australian government sent them some Tasmanian trees.

Now, unless it was our way of saying we hoped the wedding night would bring wood and a root, that present is the equivalent of socks and jocks for Christmas. At the very least, we could've got them a gift voucher.

The other royal couple to get hitched recently was Charles and Camilla Parker-Bowles. Apparently the Prince's marriage proposal was inspired by *Richard III*: 'A horse, a horse, my kingdom for a horse!'

It's been a tough romantic life for Charlie, from Diana to a few years ago when he had to confront the rumours that His Royal Highness was actually His Royal Bi-Ness. (Turns out it was all just mistaken identity. Someone had spotted Charles with Camilla and assumed he was shagging a bloke.)

For those who've been living on another planet – or read *National Geographic* at the doctor's – Charles and Camilla first met at a polo match. Charles was one of the players and Camilla was one of the ponies.

Legend has it that Camilla seduced Charles by using a bawdy pick-up line: 'My great-grandmother was the mistress of your great-grandfather, so how about it?'

Subtlety has never been the hallmark of their relationship; after all, Charles once confessed to Camilla that he wanted to be her tampon –which I assume means he wanted to see her a couple of days a month.

So why didn't Charles marry Camilla in the first place? Well, the sad fact is they were victims of tradition. Charles couldn't marry Camilla because she had a 'history'. By which I mean the same sort of history that Paris Hilton has. (In fact, Paris has so much history, it runs to several editions.)

According to tradition, the Prince must marry a virgin, or as it says in Latin on the Royal Coat Of Arms, 'Once bedded, can't be wedded.' (That's why he was sent to school in Geelong; his parents knew he'd never find a virgin there.) So instead of marrying the woman he loved, Charles hooked up with Diana because she was able to wear white to the wedding.

Hopefully his marriage to Camilla will last longer than that ill-fated affair. Though it wasn't the classic fairytale wedding, Charles's second marriage was a different type of fairytale: the one where the handsome Prince decides to marry one of the ugly stepsisters.

Also to get married recently was Avril Lavigne (aka Mini Alanis) who hooked up with Deryck Whibley of punk band Sum 41.

Wow, won't they make horrible music together? Their children will be begging for mercy during bedtime lullabies. If you think I'm being harsh, remember, this is a woman who got famous for singing 'He was a skater boy, I said see ya later boy!' Well, eat your heart out, Les Murray; I'm sure you've never thought to rhyme 'boy' with 'boy'.

But the real losers are today's kids who are growing up with celebrities like Avril and Britney as role models. The effects may not be evident now, but it's not hard to imagine *Wheel of Fortune* in 2020 when a contestant says: 'Excuse me, Steve, can I have an 8 for sk8er please?'

And while we're on the topic, did you see who McDonald's in France have chosen to front their new McCrappy-Meal campaign? The Olsen twins.

Now I don't want to be insensitive, but isn't that like getting Amanda Vanstone to advertise salad? Or Jessica Simpson to promote university admission?

While I can't blame the Olsens for taking the McTruckload of McCash, what were Maccas thinking? Is the theme of their new campaign, 'McDonald's, it tastes as good on the way back up? It's puke-time now'?

Let's face it, to Ashley and Mary-Kate, a Quarter Pounder isn't a burger, it's their weight. How about starring in an ad with Rebecca Gibney asking people for money so they can eat? Anyway, I've heard the twins prefer KFC because it comes with that handy bucket.

But while the Olsens advertising food might seem bizarre, it's nothing compared to the news that Paris Hilton has written a book.

Paris Hilton, author. It's hard to process, isn't it? It's like discovering that David Beckham co-wrote Stephen Hawking's *A Brief History of Time*. Finding Ms Bangkok Hilton in a bookshop is like running into the Pope at a brothel.

What I can't understand is all the criticism that Paris's book *Tongue in Chic: Confessions of an Heiress* is more pictures than words. I mean, what did people expect, *War and Peace*? I admit if I found a pop-up centrefold in Thomas Keneally's latest I might be shocked, but we're talking about the woman who had sex with Millsy from *Australian Idol*. (While Shannon Noll was in the background singing 'What About Me?')

And while I certainly don't approve of her fame and influence, I do think that Paris cops a lot of flak because people are simply jealous. Face it, this is a woman who is worth $20 million, doesn't have a job, and goes around the world having sex with strangers. You know what? If I had $20 million, I would do that too. Hey, let's be honest, I'd probably do it for a handful of change, and an all-day bus pass.

One celebrity I don't envy – in fact she has all my sympathy – is Katie Holmes. With Douglas Wood now released from captivity, can we turn our attention to liberating someone who really has been taken hostage by a crazed extremist?

I still can't quite believe that the virginal 26-year-old (yep, I also thought the only 26-year-old virgins these days were flight attendants) got married to Tom Cruise. Apparently it was her childhood dream come true; just before announcing the wedding, she confessed that when she was growing up, she had a poster of Tom Cruise on her bedroom wall. She said, 'I think every little girl dreams about [her wedding]. I used to think I was going to marry Tom Cruise.' Yes, Katie, but that doesn't mean you had to do it. When I was little, I dreamed about marrying Bugs Bunny when he dressed up as a girl, and my best man was going to be Batman.

Did Katie really think through all the consequences of being Holmes Alone with Tom? Does she really want to be known as Katie Cruise? Sounds to me like a holiday package for single backpackers.

Then there's the height thing. Yet again Tiny Tom has found a woman who towers over him. (Although if he wanted to find one shorter, he'd have to hang around at jockey bars or Willy Wonka's chocolate factory. Maybe Katie is a *Snow White* fan and always wanted her very own dwarf; now she has one called Teethy.)

But their height isn't the only gap between them. Holmes is sixteen years younger than Cruise, and while that doesn't mean he'll be putting a down-payment on the Neverland Ranch, I was amused to read that Brooke Shields offered him two tickets to her play, an adult for him and a child for Katie.

Of course, that was before their baby daughter was born, the naming of which confirmed what most of us had suspected all along: That either one or both of the kid's parents are completely nutty.

Suri? Are you serious? It's no coincidence that it rhymes with 'sue me' because that's what the poor little tacker will do to her parents once she's saved enough pocket-money to hire a lawyer. (If you say it quickly, it also sounds alarmingly like 'sewerage'; perhaps they named her after what her dad speaks in most of his interviews.)

The name has certainly been a talking point amongst the rich and powerful. John Howard was about to mention the birth to his Aboriginal friends but then realised he can't say the 's' word.

The shame is, if they'd wanted to give the kid a truly memorable name, they had so many alternatives. What about 'Three-hour' Cruise? Or 'Booze' Cruise? Or even 'Pleasure' Cruise?

There's been no confirmation yet on whether Katie fulfilled Tom's wishes and gave birth silently. (Is he a scientologist or a librarian?)

Personally, I think women should be free to make as much noise as they want during birth; surely pushing something that big through such a small space should be the plot for *Mission Impossible 4*? But if scientologists could get people to be quiet at the movies, I might join up.

I do wish the TomKats all the best with their bundle of joy because it will certainly be tough to discipline her. Told to stop jumping up and down on the bed, she'll retort: 'But Mum, Daddy did it on Oprah!' (Well, not exactly *on* Oprah, though that would be something I'd pay to see.)

The mini couch-jumper could have an equally naughty and strangely named playmate-in-the-making. Brad and Angelina have dipped their sticky fingers into the Scrabble letters and named their new daughter Shiloh Nouvel.

Press reports claimed Angelina had a drug-free birth, but obviously the same criteria didn't apply when it came to thinking up baby names.

Although they were nearly pipped at the wacky post by The Artist Formerly Known As Ginger Spice, Geri Halliwell, who named her daughter Bluebell Madonna Halliwell. Well I guess we all know now why she wasn't called Brain Surgery Spice. Yes Bluebell Halliwell. It's like she's a character from a Dr Seuss novel. I guess it's better than what most of the kids will call her – like You Smell Halliwell.

Apparently she chose the name Bluebell because she wanted something rare. If that's true she should have called her kid 'Quality Australian Drama Series', 'South Sydney Rabbitos Victory' or 'English Person With Straight Teeth' Halliwell.

And she went with Madonna in honour of one of her heroines. I don't know about you, but Bluebell Madonna sounds more like a name you would come up with after too much heroin.

But enough about Desperate-Cry-For-Attention Spice, and back to Baby Brangelina.

Apparently the Jolie-Pitts went with the name Shiloh after Brad's initial suggestions of Jennifer, Gwyneth or Brad 2: This Time It's Personal were rejected.

The big question now is, will being burdened with a name that sounds like someone with a lisp trying to pronounce Silo make baby Brangelina Jolie, or will she think it's the Pitts?

According to experts Shiloh is Hebrew for Messiah, and Australian for 'wow, you are going to get a whole lot of wedgies at Primary School!'

But I guess with a last name like Pitt, she would have already copped the nickname 'Arm', or for *90210* fans 'Peach'.

(And seeing Angelina already has two adopted children called Maddox and Zahara, if they had given their kid a normal name she just wouldn't have felt part of the family.)

Of course, if Shiloh grows up to have anything like the long and varied sexual history of her Mum it won't be long before she gets dubbed Not-So-Shy-Ho.

So what about Shiloh's middle-name Nouvel, which means 'new' in French. Yep, that's right, they've essentially called their daughter the New Messiah. Why didn't they just go the whole hog and call her the New and Improved Messiah, Our Messiah Kicks The Old Messiah's Arse, or I Can't Believe It's Not Buddha? (It would have been a hell of a lot worse if Ang had hung on for a couple more weeks and she'd been born on 6/6/06. Of course on that date any name but Damien is considered a good one.)

The new parents are not the only ones going over the top, some news reports even dubbed it 'the most anticipated birth since Jesus'. Although from my limited Bible studies I'm pretty sure Jesus' birth came as a surprise, even to Joseph.

And the government of Namibia, where the baby was born, even shut off the borders, closed airspace, and allowed armed guards to protect the baby from locals and press. Wow, George Bush should stop sending troops to Iraq, and just send Brad and Ang over there to squeeze out their next puppy.

They even had a no-fly zone enforced over the hospital, and also a no-Jennifer-Aniston-movies-or-old-episodes-of-*Friends*-zone on local TV.

Anyway, I wish the little tacker all the best, and I just hope for her first birthday Brad and Ang have a pool party where they serve milk for the kids, and maybe a surprise appearance by Jennifer Lopez. Then Shiloh could drink Milo on a lilo bought at Bi-Lo with J-Lo.

But the Oscar for the worst-named kid in Hollywood has got to go to ... Gwyneth Paltrow and Chris Martin, for their baby Apple.

Yes, that's right, Apple Martin. It sounds like they got pissed and misspelt a cocktail name, doesn't it? What are they going to call their next child, Victoria Bitter? 'Hi, I'd like to introduce you to our son Long-Slow-Comfortable-Screw-Up-Against-a-Wall-Paltrow-Martin.'

So why Apple? Did she have worms? Does she have a Granny called Smith? Was she born with a little sticker on her head? Was it because they washed her and then dried her, or was she just so damned cute they wanted to eat her up?

Maybe they chose the moniker because when Martin first saw her he got a lump in his throat, or maybe she just seemed to keep the doctors away?

Perhaps when Chris got Gwynnie preggers he thought he had planted the wrong seed? Or possibly they just wanted to see the newspaper headline: 'Woman Gives Birth to Apple.'

One popular theory claimed the name is a tribute to Gwyneth's home town of New York. The kid should consider herself lucky that Gwynnie doesn't hail from Rooty Hill or Pakenham Upper.

Naming your child after a city has long been a celebrity favourite. West Indies cricket great Brian Lara famously named his baby girl Sydney after he scored a double-century at the SCG. I guess she's pretty lucky he wasn't playing in Lahore.

Then there was Posh and Becks who named their child Brooklyn after where he was conceived. Of course, since Beckham started letting his fingers do the porking, I guess the kid should be grateful it wasn't named Vodafone or STD.

Personally, I'm grateful my parents didn't choose the 'place of conception' option. I doubt American Express would've let me put In-the-Back-of-a-Ute-After-a-B-and-S-Ball Anderson on my credit card.

One rumour suggested Apple was named after a line in a Coldplay song, but if that's the case, surely they would've chosen something 'Yellow'. (Although I guess Lemon might've caused a few problems.)

One source even suggested she was named after Apple computers, which is cruel to say the least, because at school she'll be incompatible with most of the other children.

Let's face it, as well as guaranteeing she'll never marry Johnny Rotten, Chris and Gwyn have condemned young Apple to a lifetime of teasing.

Her nickname will always be 'muffin'. Teenage boys will 'pine' for her and constantly be trying to get her to 'turnover', and in maths she'll be the first one asked to define 'pi'. (Yes, it will be pun-demonium.)

In fact, with all the teasing, she'll be lucky not to 'crumble' or end up a 'fruit cake'. (Although on the upside, with a name like Apple she'll make her teachers happy just by coming to class.)

But seriously, burdening your kid with a stupid name seems to be a favourite celebrity sport these days. The Geldofs and Zappas apparently named their kids by pulling random letters out of a Scrabble bag.

Naked Chef Jamie Oliver must've been cooking up a recipe for mull cake when he named his daughters Daisy-Boo and Poppy-Honey. I'm starting to wonder whether those long white lines on his kitchen table are actually salt.

Sure, they might be cute now, but what will happen when the kids grow up and want to be taken seriously? Who wants to get on a plane and hear: 'Hi, this is your captain Daisy-Boo speaking!'

Meanwhile, singer Toni Braxton has a child called Denim, which I guess has to do with genes; Christie Brinkley's daughter is condemned to a lifetime of 'hello Sailor'; and John Travolta's kid Jett (is this another case of where the baby was conceived?) will hope his dad's connection with Qantas doesn't mean he has to change his name to Jetstar.

Rachel Griffith's son Banjo must've been conceived after a particularly good pluck; Billy-Ray Cyrus's child should Achy Breaky his face for burdening her with Destiny Hope; and don't even get me started on *Northern Exposure*'s Rob Morrow calling his daughter Tu.

Come to think of it, perhaps the name Apple does have some appeal. And let's face it, with a surname like Martin, it could've been a whole lot worse: for starters, consider Aston, Remy, Ricky or God forbid, Ray.

SEVEN

WWW.DUMB.COM

Did the person who came up with the name 'banker' get the first letter wrong?

Before I am beaten to death with the 'next teller please' sign, I should clarify that I am not talking about the humble bank staff here. I realise that working in a bank must be like being a bouncer at a strip-club: you get to stare at the good stuff all day but can never take any of it home. (At least when you work at a fancy restaurant you sometimes score a doggy-bag.)

No, I'm talking about the big boys who make massive profits at our expense and never pass any of it back to the consumers. In fact, while services decrease, costs rise. Most banks these days have less branches than a Tasmanian family tree, and yet the list of fees on my monthly statement reads longer than Paris Hilton's latest book.

My last update included so many different charges, I thought I'd accidentally received Keith Richards' mini-bar bill. Sometimes the fees are so ridiculous, I'm tempted to ask the teller to wear a balaclava so I can get the full experience of being robbed.

The truth is, the banks are making huge profits, and if you'd invested in bank shares ten years ago, you'd have made much more money than if you'd kept your dosh in one of their accounts. Sadly, most people are scared that if they question the fees, their next statement will include a 'complaining about the fees fee'.

And what is the deal with bank opening hours? While every other business is working towards 24/7, the banks seem to be open between 11 and 11.15 every second Tuesday and only if you bring a boiled egg and say the code-word 'jam trousers'.

Every time I go into my local bank, the lines are longer than what you'd find on Robert Downey Jnr's glass-top table. In fact, only once in my life have I gone into a bank to find no one else there. The shock nearly caused me to drop my shotgun and bite through the stocking on my head.

And I'm even less impressed by these new banks where you have to take a number. I'm sorry, I didn't realise I was at a deli. Can I have some cash, and a stick of cabanossi?

But you'd forgive all this if it made it easier to get your money. But it doesn't. Most cheques take more time to clear than Mamdouh Habib's passport.

Why is it that when I pay a cheque to someone, the money is taken out of my account immediately, but when someone pays me a cheque I have to wait five days for it to clear? What happens to that money in the meantime? I suspect there is a little room out the back where bank staff get naked and roll around in our cash.

I concede that with personal cheques, they do need to make sure you have the money, but why do bank cheques take three days to clear? I can understand why they might not trust me, but do they really need three days to check if St George has $2000? Are they worried that Julie Anthony and the Dragon have been on a massive bender and spent all the cash?

The truth is, they don't want us in the banks. They want us to use ATMs and phone banking.

Personally, I have no problem with ATMs, but older bank users complain that they don't understand the new technology – although, to be honest, if you've ever seen an oldie at the pokies they seem to understand the new technology very well.

Maybe that's what the banks should do: just combine the two. Once you've put in your PIN and request for cash, a little message would flash on the screen saying, 'Go on, double or nothing.'

Phone banking, on the other hand, really pisses me off. Just for once I would like to talk to a real person rather than a machine. If I wanted to hear someone talk to me in a computerised voice I would prank-call Stephen Hawking.

'You have been placed in a queue. Please hold, your call is very important to us.' Yeah, right! Can't you just tell the truth? I'd have more respect for the bank if the recorded message said: 'We couldn't give a crap about your call. We already have your money. Press hash to end the call or just hang up.'

While we're on the topic of computerised voices, what the hell's with Telstra and their misleadingly named Directory Assistance service. (A better name would be 'Don't Call Us, We'll Call You!')

First they changed the number from the very simple 013 to something that even Rainman has to write on the back of his hand. The only way to get connected these days is to enter pi to twenty decimal places.

You know they are trying to stop your calls when you have to ring Directory Assistance to get the number for Directory Assistance.

But that's not even the worst bit of the new 'service'. No, I'm talking about the new and improved (cough, cough) computerised voice-recognition. My God, voice-recognition! It's about as misleading a name as *Australia's Funniest Home Videos*.

Just who is the genius who took a perfectly good system – where you spoke to a real, live person who would tell you the number you wanted – and replace it with a computer that seems to have been programmed by the writers of *Burgo's Catch Phrase*?

I mean, if they insisted on sacking people in favour of a computer-generated voice, they could've at least made it a cool one, like Yoda's. 'Hmmm, seek the Hut of Pizza you do? Here the number is! But remember pineapple, egg, a pizza needs not these things. These are the way to the dark side!'

At the very least, is it too much to ask for a system that actually works better, rather than one that replaces people's jobs with a machine that makes a simple phone call more difficult than conversing with a drunk, dyslexic Salvador Dali?

Seriously, have you tried to use this craputer? You request something simple like 'Bunning's Warehouse' and the technology translates it into, 'Did you say Purple Monkey Dishwasher?' No I didn't. But now I feel like I'm on acid. The other day I asked for the number of ABC Radio Melbourne and it replied, 'Did you say Frankston Midget Lesbian Bikini Waxing Service?' No I did not . . . but on second thoughts, put me through.

While it's novel to experience what it might be like to talk to Ozzy Osbourne, I have become so frustrated with this 'lack of service' that the other day I tried to be clever and head it off at the pass. As soon as the message kicked in, I screamed 'Operator!'. But the stupid computer simply replied: 'I'm sorry, I did not understand your request. Please hold for an operator.'

(My next few words would have made Shane Warne blush. The funny thing is, after hearing my tirade, the computer promptly gave me the home number for Russell Crowe.)

Come on people, let's call a spade a spade – and not what the Directory Assistance would call it: 'Did you say a banana?' – Dexter from *Perfect Match* had a better strike-rate than that stupid Telstra computer. So the question has to be asked: how do they get away with it?

The answer is simple: We let them.

Well, no more. Frankly, I'm sick of it. I'm mad as hell and I'm not going to take it anymore. It's time to send big business a message, and if you're with me, here's what you do: Don't pay your Telstra bill.

Stick with me, I'm serious, don't pay it; it's the only way they will learn, money is the only language they understand. A month from now you'll get a reminder notice, with five dollars added on (because that's how much a stamp costs in Telstra land) but hold firm, don't pay. A month later, you'll receive another notice, then another, and then a final notice.

This is where the fun starts, because this is when they call you. 'Hello, it's Cindy from Telstra. You haven't paid your Telstra bill, you owe us $165.'

That's when you say: 'Did you say two avocados and a chip packet? By the way, did I mention your call was very important to me?' And then hang up.

Which reminds me: Is there anything more annoying than unwanted phone calls at home? I have a girlfriend who gets between ten and twenty a night, and that's not even telemarketers, that's just Warnie.

But it's true, sales calls and surveys can really ruin a pleasant, quiet meal with your family. I mean, often you even have to turn down the TV.

It seems these days that every time you pick up the receiver, someone is trying to sell you something. I'm starting to suspect the only reason ET wanted to phone home was because Optus was offering a really good deal on intergalactic calls.

It's gotten so bad that during a séance the other night, a friend of mine was contacted by Big Kev who said he was 'dead but still excited' – and then tried to sell him some goo remover.

Anyway, after receiving a few calls of their own, the government has finally had enough, and is proposing to fix the problem with a 'Do not call' register.

(John Howard and his senior advisers have had the same system for years: they didn't call him about the AWB, they didn't call him about the WMDs, they didn't call him about the children overboard.)

Basically, those with hang-up hang-ups will be able to sign this register. Then, if a telemarketer calls, the company will be liable for fines of up to $200,000. And if that doesn't stop them, the government will send Russell Crowe over – and you can just imagine the damage he could do in a room filled with phones.

The new system will mainly target telemarketers, but why stop there? Why not bring in a register for friends and family too?

You could have a 'Do not call me at ten o'clock on a Sunday morning Mum, I have a hangover' register. Or a 'Do not call me if I owe you money' register. Or a 'Do not call me Grandma if you're just going to bang on about how I don't call you enough, or how Uncle Alan's swollen knee really looks like Bert Newton' register.

And for the ladies, how about a 'Do not booty call' register to protect you from 2 a.m. calls from your ex begging for sex; or random calls from drunk rugby league players?

While I understand that a series of unwanted calls could provoke even the gentlest person to shove the receiver in a place with no reception, I actually have the reverse problem. You see, I have never been called by a telemarketer.

Yes, that's right. Not once. Ever. Before you go green with envy, consider for a moment how unpopular you'd feel if even people in Indian call centres don't want to talk to you.

No one has ever tried to sell me something, beg me to donate, asked me where I stand on the Jolie/Aniston issue, or got me to answer a survey about whether Kim Beazley would be more popular if he wore a sports bra.

Maybe I *do* have some opinions on LPG v petrol. Maybe I *would* like to apply for a low-interest credit card. Maybe I *would* like to give money to an obscure charity like 'Machine Guns for Monkeys'. But sadly, no one will ever know.

Hey, I'd even settle for one of those pre-recorded messages John Howard sent out before the last election. (Mostly because it would have given me an opportunity to say what I really think of him without being locked up for sedition.)

A part of me actually suspects we may be looking at this whole thing the wrong way. If people are irritated by these calls, maybe we don't need to ban them, perhaps they should just be less annoying.

Instead of the calls coming from an Indian call centre, how about if they were made by phone-sex operators? Instead of paying $4.95 a minute, at the end you'd only have to buy a series of cut-price beauty products, or change your phone server . . . change it now! (If they employed sadomasochists, customer abuse would no longer be an issue.)

But here's how it could get really sinister. We've all heard of subliminal advertising and product placement in movies, how soon before these companies start paying your friends and family to do their selling?

'Wil, it's Nanna. How is your health dear? Because you know MBF has discounted health packages available . . . By the way, I'd love you to call me more often ... which you could do if you switched to Vodafone who are offering half-price calls after six.'

The frustrations of phone communication can probably account for the huge popularity of email.

I, for one, am addicted to turning on the computer and seeing, 'You have a new message.' It's been about one minute now since I last logged on, and already my mouse-finger is getting shaky.

The funny thing is, I'm not really sure what the appeal of email is. After all, despite all its drawbacks, we have had a far superior invention around for decades; it's called 'the phone'.

I guess part of the fascination is that email is new, like iPods or most of Kerry-Anne Kennerley's face; whereas the phone is old, like the steam-engine or Daryl Somers' jokes.

If email had been around for fifty years, and we'd just invented the phone, then everyone would be saying: 'Hey Gary, you've got to check out this new invention, it's amazing. It's just like email, but you can actually talk to the person.'

That said, nowadays they're inventing more and more phones you can type on, so what the hell do I know? I'm pretty sure if you give the latest Vodafone to a thousand monkeys, they'll eventually SMS you the complete works of William Shakespeare – or at least send David Beckham a dirty textie.

But the truth is, I have become totally reliant on the internet, or as those in the know call it, the World Wide Web. (Not that it is completely worldwide; I doubt there are too many kids in Ethiopia logging onto www.food.com.)

That said, there are a couple of things that bother me about the World Wide Web, and not just that its abbreviation www has more syllables than the full name.

My first problem is the prevalence of adult content on the Net. It's made it virtually impossible to look up anything without being directed to a porn site.

The other day I was trying to build a shelf for the house and innocently Googled 'wood' 'screws' and 'jugs'. Before I knew it, I was directed to sites that were less hardware and more hard-core. (Many of which featured Paris Hilton.)

But even worse is a plague that has started to impinge on the joy of email – spam. Yes, this insidious group mailing has clogged my inbox so badly that it needs constant cleaning out. To some it might sound like my inbox needs two weeks on the All-Bran diet, but I'm actually referring to those ads for products like Penis Enlarging Pills and Generic Viagra guaranteed to get you harder than Ray Martin's hair.

Seriously, in the last couple of months I've been offered so much generic Viagra, I could make the Leaning Tower of Pisa stand up straight.

But does anyone really buy generic medicine over the internet? What's next? Swapping pills on eBay? I won't even buy Home-Brand toilet paper, let alone a case of Generic Valium from www. swallowthisidareyou.com.

And did I mention the porn? Now I don't mind the ones that are easily identifiable as porn, it's the ones that trick you that really bother me. You're in a busy office opening an attachment you thought was a lovely shot of girls having fun on a farm, but it's actually a scene from *McLeod's Daughters Uncut*.

Even worse are the ones with headers like: 'A message from a friend you haven't heard from in a while.' Then you open it up to discover it's not from a long-lost friend because if you had any friends who could do the things in the photos, let's face it, they'd hear from you all the time.

Speaking of unwanted letters from 'friends', my other pet hate is chain mail.

Personally I think there is a special corner in hell for people who forward chain letters, especially the ones that threaten bad luck if you don't pass them on.

What sort of friend sends you something that reads: 'If you don't do what I say, bad things are going to happen to you'? Well, unless your friend's email is osama@hiddencave.com.

And the threats are always so weird. 'Mr John Smith of Made-upville refused to pass on this letter, so for the rest of his life he suffered from really bad hat-hair, even when he hadn't been wearing a hat. A man from Adelaide refused to send on this chain letter, and he still lives in Adelaide.'

'Kim Beazley refused to send on this email, and was punished by becoming leader of the ALP not once, not twice but on three separate occasions. Tremble at the power of the letter.'

'Another man trashed this email. Shortly after, he was forced to listen to Daryl Somers' new album over and over and over again. He was then stabbed to death in his sleep – which actually came as a relief because it put an end to Daryl Somers.'

What I do love in these stories is how quickly someone's

fortune can change: 'An oil tycoon called George received this email and didn't pass it on. He immediately lost his fortune, was then captured by aliens who probed him and feasted on his brains, until they dropped him back on earth a brainless zombie.

'Now brain-dead, he forwarded the email on to his friends, and two days later he was elected president of the USA.'

Of course, as anyone with even half a brain might ask: If a person didn't pass on the letter, and then they died in tragic circumstances, how did people make the connection?

I've never seen that episode of *CSI*. 'We've ruled out murder, accidental death and suicide, it can only be one thing . . . didn't respond to a chain letter!'

They are complete crapola, and I don't care how many exclamation marks, dollar signs or block capitals are in the letter. In fact, the more desperate they are for you to believe the claim, the more exclamation marks they put on the end!!!!!!!!! Who is writing these things, the former editors of *Smash Hits*! magazine?????

Oh, and regardless of the subject of the letter, it was always started by monks. I think the theory goes that if you make its origins convoluted and spiritual, people will buy anything. This is pretty much the secret behind all three *Matrix* films.

I'm sorry, but if you truly believe a letter can change your luck, then how do you manage to leave the house in the morning? Aren't you paralysed by the fear of walking under a ladder, coming across a black cat, breaking a mirror or stepping on a crack in the sidewalk?

Answer me this: If chain letters are really so powerful, why have I never seen an Academy Award winner say: 'I'd like to thank the director, my co-stars and my agent, but the real reason for my success is that Getting to Know You email I sent on the other day.'

And you know what? I don't give a toss if it's been around the world five times. So has Catriona Rowntree but does that mean I should send her to five of my mates? (Though some of them might consider that lucky.)

Yep, there's no doubt that email is used for the dodgiest things these days. Would you believe that the other week I received an email inviting me to join a cult? And I'm not talking about the Kiss Army, Amway or the Daddos, but a genuine Doomsday, End-of-the-World, Apocalypse, Get-Your-Gear-Off, Give-Us-All-Your-Money, Oh-Crap-We're-All-Gonna-Die cult.

I still remember the good old days when most cults feared technology, and even refused to use ATMs because they believed 666 was the PIN of the Beast; when Apple was Eve's snack in the Garden of Eden; Y2K the latest fragrance from Calvin Klein; and Silicon Valley was that weird gap between Tori Spelling's breasts.

Anyway, after reading the rather bewildering email, I wasn't inspired to sign up. But it did get me thinking about a few tips for anyone considering starting their very own apocalypse cult.

Okay, let's start with the pitch. If you want people to join your cult the initial pitch is all-important. You've got to emphasise all the good points up front and play down the bad stuff – kind of like what they do to sell low-fat chips. They bang a massive sticker up the top that says '97 per cent fat-free', and down the bottom in tiny, almost illegible print a warning that reads, 'May cause anal leakage.'

Point number two: Make sure you mention the group sex; that always seems to be a pretty strong selling point.

Which brings us, inevitably, to the whole 'apocalyptic' thing. As a doomsday cult, at some point you'll have to predict the end of the world, if only to justify the name.

But if you are going to predict the destruction of humanity, then at least make it a good few years in the future, because if your predicted date comes and the world doesn't end, well it'll pretty hard to regain your credibility. 'Oh, what's that? Did I say today? No, I meant next week. This is a nine, not a six . . . Gee, I wish God had clearer handwriting.' If you think John Farnham lost a bit of cred when he kept doing gigs after his 'The Last Time' tour, then imagine being a cult leader who has predicted the end of the world, but then has to front up again three months later with the 'End of the World Tour 2, with special guest Tom Jones'.

Speaking of predictions, I'd advise the budding cult leader to have a solid source for their nutty rantings. The Bible is very popular, although any religious text will do. (Please note, Steve Waugh's tour diaries don't carry this qualification outside Australia.)

And finally, if you want your cult to really take off, then I suggest you invest in a compound. Think Playboy Mansion rather than that hole in the ground where they found Saddam.

Or take your inspiration from the *Big Brother* house: somewhere where your followers can hang out, have loads of wild sex, and be told what to do. (And after observing it for three weeks, most people will hope the army attacks with tanks and tear gas.)

Which reminds me: Have you been watching that show? I have to confess I haven't seen a minute of it. If I wanted to watch brain-dead bogans get blind on Bacardi Breezer, I'd move back into my uni share-house.

But I did catch a picture of one of the evictees in *Ralph* magazine, and as I am a big brother myself, I reckon that makes me about as qualified as most other media commentators to bang on about it.

According to moral crusaders and various letters to the editor, *Big Brother* just keeps getting ruder. Yes, it seems when they named it *Big Brother Uncut*, they were actually referring to the uncircumcised men in the shower. One scribe even dubbed it 'Big Brothel' and described it as a 'month-long masturbation fest' – which was also the tagline used to advertise the Melbourne International Film Festival.

Liberal morals campaigner Trish Draper went a step further recently and is now rallying against 'promiscuous behaviour, binge-drinking, simulated sex scenes, full frontal nudity and lewd and suggestive acts'. But enough about Warnie, what does she think about *Big Brother*?

Ms Draper said that in her opinion, *Big Brother* isn't entertainment. (Although it must be said that her definitions tend to differ from most of society's; after all what we called a 'taxpayer-funded overseas holiday with her boyfriend' she named a 'study tour'. Oh well, you say tomato, we say travel rort.)

Peek-through-the-Draper demanded a probe into the show –

although wasn't all the excess probing the source of the complaints in the first place?

She also branded the show a moral outrage, which is a little rich coming from a government that locks kids in detention centres.

'Hi, you have called the kettle. I'm not in right now, but if this is Trish Draper, who are you calling black?'

Look, to be honest, there is plenty about *Big Brother* that offends me too – not least Gretel Killeen's fashion sense – but I have a pretty straightforward solution. I don't watch. Why don't all these outraged people simply change the channel? Or perhaps they don't have a hand free?

If we are really worried about the messages we are sending our kids, then what about the 450 *CSI* shows that all start with a dead body? Stiffs are okay but not stiffies? Is that it?

To quote that great philosopher, Lleyton Hewitt: Come on! If a couple of nude people on TV were that offensive, SBS would've been out of business years ago.

My only complaint about *Big Brother* is that it regularly runs over fifteen minutes late. Who is doing the programming at Channel Ten? The bloke who runs Sydney trains?

The reason it runs overtime, I reckon, is because the program contains so much offensive material that the pre-show warning goes for fifteen minutes. I swear the voice-over guy was puffing the other night.

But what's this about 'discussion of adult themes'? Does it refer to talk of interest rates and the price of real estate? Let's be honest, when these bogans open their mouths they make *The Footy Show* look like the Algonquin Round Table.

While you couldn't pay me to watch them, I think it's great these warm yellow puddles in the shallow end of the gene pool are locked in the house. It means I have less chance of running into them. In fact, instead of voting them out, we should vote bogans *in* and when the house is full, bulldoze it.

Which is what I wish I could've done to my old house before I vacated the place. You see, I expended so much energy trying to get my bond back, it would've been easier to report that the whole place had gone up in smoke than explain each and every carpet stain, broken window and leaky tap.

'That stain on the rug? Yes, of course I can explain that. You see there was a massive storm, and the roof leaked. Did I mention it was raining bong water?'

'And you're never going to believe this, but that same night we were robbed, and the burglars not only took our stuff, they stuck posters all over the walls . . . with Blu-Tack!'

'What's that? The grafitti on the roof that says *Wil Rulz*? I'm pretty sure that was there when we moved in!'

But despite my best efforts, I knew I was fighting a losing battle when my real estate agent informed me that M. Night Shymalan was going to use my bathroom as the setting for his next horror film.

I should've guessed that she was never going to believe that the pile of garbage in the corner was modern art, and the rats crawling in it were critics. (Oh, the hours I wasted pasting berets to their little heads!)

But apart from developing your creativity, the other thing you learn when moving house is just who your real friends are. If Jesus felt betrayed when Peter denied him three times, it's a good thing he never asked him to hook a trailer to the donkey to help move mangers.

Some so-called friends just refuse to help point-blank, and then there are the others who agree to help, but it's like making a deal with Don Corleone from *The Godfather*: 'Yes, I will help you move, but someday I will call upon you to do a service for me.'

So finally, after trying to stuff your car tighter than Alex Lloyd at an all-you-can-eat buffet, you realise your Holden Barina is not meant to look like a Holden Pinjata and you decide to hire professionals.

While this is certainly a weight off your back, it's not a weight off your mind, because is it just me, or do all removalists look like they've just come out of prison?

Although I guess it does make sense for them to be ex-cons. They already know how to enter someone's house to take stuff; all they have to remember is to put the goods back again. (And to avoid driving past Cash Converters.)

You might think I'm being a bit harsh, but the blokes who helped me move could be evidence of the missing link.

They say if you put a thousand monkeys in a room with a thousand typewriters, they will eventually write the entire works of Shakespeare. If you put a thousand removalists in a room with a thousand typewriters, they might eventually bash out an episode of *The Footy Show*.

Anyway, after spending a couple of hours picking nits off each other, they did eventually get the job done. So all that remained for me to do was drop off the keys at the real estate agent.

Just as one of the rules of the universe is that toast will always land butter side down, it's also true that you will invariably give the real estate agent many more keys than you were given.

(The next renters will also get the keys to my car, to my grand-mother's jewellery box, to the million-dollar suitcase on *Deal Or No Deal*, to a cupboard that leads to the magical kingdom of Narnia, and one I picked out of a bowl at a very fun party.)

Though I'm the first to admit we really needed to move – our flat was so small, if you got an erection you had to open a window – I am going to miss the old place. After all, it's the place I've called 'home'. In some ways, it's almost like splitting with a girlfriend:

'Look it's not you, it's me. We had some great times together. I loved the way you let me fall asleep inside you every night, and how sometimes we'd even invite my friends over too.

'I loved how, even after I'd been on the road sleeping in cheap hotel rooms, you'd always take me back. You didn't need to put a chocolate on your pillow to make me feel welcome. Sure I was renting you by the week, but it never felt like that to me.

'But I think we both know it's time for a change. I want to be free to see other apartments, houses, bed-sits, and if I'm in the mood maybe even a twin-share.

'And don't worry, you'll find someone else too. Sure, you're a little older, a little more run-down (although I'm certain that saggy floor was there when I moved in) but you'll be seeing someone new before you know it. If you have any trouble, maybe you could put an ad in the paper. After all, that's how we met!'

One person who isn't vacating his home in a hurry is John Howard. Despite our strongest wishes for a new tenant at Kirribilli House, one thing's for sure: he'll die before he gives up his post. Let's not forget that we're talking about a man who didn't leave home until he was 32.

This is a man who, in the '60s, when everyone else was out looking for casual sex, was at home trying to find some casual socks . . . to wear with his sandals. While all the cool kids were wearing tie-dye, John was wearing a tie. Forget LSD, he was into GST; the only trips he took were to local Young Liberals meetings.

Not that you'd want John Howard as your flatmate. Can you imagine it? What a downer (and I'm not talking about when his mate Alexander popped around).

He'd constantly promise to take the bins out, and then claim it was a non-core promise when he didn't do so. Even though he had the downstairs bedroom, he'd forever be trying to get control of the upper part of the house; and he'd spend hours in the bathroom with nothing but his Steve Waugh autobiography.

And is it just me, or does our beloved PM strike you as the sort of bloke who'd label his food in the fridge but still climb into yours? And speaking of food, he'd definitely ban lattes, and don't even think about opening a bottle of chardonnay, you socialist.

And you'd be condemned to eat cold, stale pizza because John would lock the delivery boys in the garage for six months before letting them into the house.

As in many share-houses, the stereo would also be a sticking point. Forget about Leftfield, Billy Bragg or The Whitlams, John would refuse to move the dial from Alan Jones.

And don't even get me started on the phone. You'd go to make a call only to discover that John had actually sold the phone and was now going to charge you to buy it back.

But there would also be some upsides to sharing a house with the PM. For starters, displaying take-away menus on the fridge would be easy because the entire thing would be crawling with terrorism hotline magnets.

And if you ever had to sell anything, John would organise a $50 million advertising campaign to help you along.

Also, one of John's greatest attributes is his cleanliness. Indeed, he spends the good part of most days compulsively washing his hands of the smallest trace of dirt.

Unfortunately, though, he doesn't apply the same standards to the rest of the house. If there is a stain on the carpet, first he will deny that the stain exists; then he will claim he was never notified about it; and finally he'll say the carpet is actually better off with the stain, and there's no way he will apologise to the owners.

Anyway, I have to go now. There seem to be some big, boofy blokes in black suits and dark sunnies banging on my door and yelling something about sedition. I hope they aren't mistaking me for the latest recruit to Al-Qaeda.

Yes, didn't you hear? Another terrorist tape hit the news recently, and this time the star was an Aussie.

Well, to be fair, the balaclava-clad bandit's accent fluctuated wildly between Australian and cockney, so officials initially suspected it was someone who'd spent too much time watching Dick Van Dyke in *Mary Poppins* or listening to interviews with Kylie Minogue.

I have to admit that when I first saw the footage on TV, I didn't even realise it was a terror tape. I heard the accent and assumed it was the new Shannon Noll film-clip.

But the bad sound quality, shaky camera work, lack of plot and dodgy dialogue convinced the authorities that it was definitely home-grown. In fact, their first suspects were the people who made *You and Your Stupid Mate*.

They also started to wonder whether the man in the balaclava might have been an Aussie when he said George W. Bush was a 'flamin' mongrel'; the Iraqi desert was 'dry as a dead dingo's donger' and then raised his gun in the air and screamed, 'That's not a knife, it's an AK-47!' Plus, even though he was wearing camouflage trousers, his arse-crack was showing; his balaclava had corks on it; and what appeared to be a grenade up his sleeve turned out to be a packet of Winnie Blues.

And as for that black camouflage war-paint on his face. Well, it all became clear when later he spread it on his toast and sang, 'I'm a happy little Terrorist!'

(Other clues included his plan to raise funds by holding a sausage sizzle and chook raffle, and then killing anyone who didn't like beetroot on their hamburger.)

Australians are so laid-back, it's hard for us to imagine how one of our own was recruited to Al-Qaeda. Well, unless they thought it was a new footy team, or free beer was involved.

Let's be honest, the average Aussie bloke doesn't care about finding WMDs, he just wants to get to the VBs; the only bombs he knows about are those you do off the diving board; he thinks the Coalition of the Willing is a threesome; and friendly fire is when you're offered a joint.

So the big question is: Who could it possibly have been? All we knew for sure was that it was someone who hadn't been seen in a while, who had a massive grudge against the Australian people, and a tendency towards violence. Did anyone check on Mark Latham?

The main theory around the traps was that the terrorist might have been an ex-Australian army soldier fighting for the other side – which is like Shane Warne suddenly bowling for England or having phone sex with his wife.

But everyone seemed to agree that he was most definitely an Aussie; so much so that we didn't claim what we normally do when one of our own embarrasses us overseas: Say he is from New Zealand.

Anyway, everyone no doubt saw the tape and made up their own mind. In fact, there was so much publicity, I've no doubt we'll see him on the next series of *Dancing with the Stars*. (Well, he couldn't be any more unpopular than Derryn Hinch.)

Next thing you know, Channel Seven will be inviting Saddam Hussein onto the program. Yep, ever since they found him in that hole – otherwise known as Adelaide – I've been waiting for him to appear on the show.

Did you know that when he was down there, he survived on a diet of Spam, hotdogs and Mars Bars? That's according to members of the Pennsylvania National Guard who watched over him in prison, and recently spoke to the media.

Apparently he also had $750,000 in cash in a suitcase. When the soldiers first found him, he should have grabbed the suitcase and yelled: 'Andrew I'm guessing $200,000 . . . Deal or no deal!'

The soldiers also revealed that Saddam 'tried to flee in a taxicab as the tanks were rolling in'. If only the US had invaded at the 3 o'clock change-over time, they would have got him straight away.

When it came to breakfast, the Butcher of Baghdad preferred cereal to fried eggs because he reckoned the latter contained too much oil and were bad for his health (funny, that). So every day, he'd munch on Raisin Bran. I guess it's better than the old days when he used to eat Kurds and whey. (Snap, Crackle and Pop was also off the menu as it brought back too many lovely memories of torturing his opponents. Speaking of which, I am sure Saddam is a great fan of Pringles: 'Once you pop [your gun, that is] you can't stop.'

Apparently Saddam is paranoid about cleanliness, and hates germs. President Bush was in total agreement. 'Yeah, I don't like those people from Germany either,' he said.

The soldiers also reported that Saddam still believes he is the president of Iraq. He must be getting advice from the former Iraqi information minister. In fact, not only is Saddam still president, Iraq won the war, and he is having a hot and steamy affair with Angelina Jolie.

When it comes to US presidents, Saddam revealed that he really misses Ronald Reagan. If George W. gets his way, Saddam can look forward to a reunion with Ronnie really soon.

Unfortunately the report didn't mention what Saddam thought of the pictures of him in his undies that were published around the world. But having examined the photos myself, I don't think he's got too much to be worried about. In fact, I think we might have finally identified where he is hiding those Weapons of Mass Destruction.

EIGHT

VOTE ONE DUMB

Did you hear that Peter Costello is the new Prime Minister of Australia? Yep, that's right, recently the Treasurer decided to announce who's boss. No, it's not John Howard, and it certainly isn't Tony Danza, apparently it's him.

Sneaky Pete said: 'I am the Treasurer; I am the deputy leader of the Liberal Party; so I feel in a sense that I do lead this country.' Yeah, in a sense; and in a sense Dame Edna is a woman.

That's like me saying: 'I am a comedian; I am on a show with Corinne Grant, so in a sense I feel that I am Rove. I have won three Gold Logies; say hi to your mum for me!'

What the . . . ? Come on, Peter, you saying you lead the country is like Andrew Ridgeley claiming to be the artistic genius behind Wham! Or Ozzie Ostrich announcing that he is the host of *Dancing with the Stars*.

It certainly must make for a confusing time in Liberal caucus meetings. First John Howard stands up and says, 'I'm the leader' then Mr Costello responds, 'No, *I'm* the leader' then someone else announces, 'No, *I* am Spartacus.'

Don't get me wrong, when the time comes for the Prime Minister to don the Vodafone trakkie fulltime, then I reckon Mr Costello is the best of a bad bunch.

Tony Abbott is too busy working on his stand-up comedy career to be much of a threat; Bronwyn Bishop doesn't get the irony in her telling young women not to wear ridiculous things on their heads; and Philip Ruddock might make a good leader if it weren't for his allergies to sunlight, garlic and holy water. (Put it this way, if Ruddock became leader of the Libs, the ALP would have to replace Beazley with Buffy.)

So sure, Mr Costello may have earned the right to be the next Liberal leader, but that's like being behind a pensioner at the ATM: you may be next in line, but you're going to be stuck there a while.

Even Peter Costello would have to admit that John Howard deserves the right to leave when he chooses, and currently his position as leader of the Libs (oops; should that 'b' be an 'e'?) has never been stronger.

He's survived children overboard, WMDs, IR, and Iraq. Voters seem to think that it's better the devil you voted for. Sure, the PM may have his faults, but what if the replacement is much, much worse? I refer the jury to the case of Ian 'Dicko' Dickson vs Kyle 'Vile' Sandilands.

And Howard's not going anywhere. In fact, a lot of people have suggested the PM might try and emulate his hero Robert Menzies who retired at 71, but I actually think he's got his eyes on the Pope.

Given his love of cricket, I wouldn't be surprised if Mr Howard is hoping to beat Bradman's average of 99.94. (By the way, what does Janette Howard say to her husband when he's at the height of passion? 'Turn off the cricket, dear, and come to bed!')

Certainly things were looking grim for Mr Costello the other day when the PM stuck a bumper-sticker on his Commonwealth car that read: 'You can have the prime ministership when you pry it from my cold, dead hands.'

One man whose dreams of lounging in the Lodge with a bucket of chicken seem further than ever is the Labor leader, Kim Beazley.

Seriously, what the hell is going on with the federal ALP? In recent polling Kim Beazley's approval ratings were lower than the waistband on Paris Hilton's hipsters. You know you are in trouble when you're out-rated not only by John Howard, but also by Jana Pittman's knee and bird flu.

If the Labor Party were a dog you would have to 'send it to the farm'. If polls freefall any further, people who haven't been born yet are still not going to vote for them.

So what are the problems? Well, for starters, the factional system is more stuffed than Kim Beazley at an all-you-can-eat buffet. It got really nasty at one stage, didn't it? It's quite amazing how dirty members of the ALP will fight for the right to lose elections.

(It's the first time I've ever heard of rats trying to jump onto a sinking ship.)

There's so much dead wood on the back benches of the ALP, I hope they have good smoke detectors at party headquarters. And there seems to be no loyalty at all. At Labor meetings, they don't play 'Follow the leader' or 'Pin the tail on the donkey', they amuse themselves with 'Follow the leader and stab him in the back!'

So inevitably, the public is left with the impression that everyone in the ALP hates each other. They don't just need decisive leadership, they need therapy.

We need a strong opposition to keep the government honest and accountable. During the Cole inquiry, if the ALP had discovered a photo of John Howard personally handing Saddam Hussein a novelty cheque for $300 million, they still would've buggered it up. I can just see it now: Kim Beazley calling a press conference to announce the news, and Simon Crean sneaking up behind him to give him a wedgie.

While I think he's doing a pretty crappy job, I do feel a bit sorry for Kim. Apparently even friends are saying he has the smell of death about him – although that could be the kebab he's stored in his pocket for afternoon tea.

But it's not as if the ALP had that many options when Latham kicked over his ladder of opportunity. When they elected Beazley as leader, I was reminded of a bad cooking show: 'None of the other candidates had the right ingredients . . . so here's one we prepared earlier.'

Kim was always going to be the front waddler for the gig. That said, the ability to stick around so long you eventually get the job doesn't necessarily make you the most talented candidate; just look at Daryl Somers.

Eventually the leadership challengers pledged to be behind Mr Beazley – but that's only because they were better positioned to stick a knife into his back.

And look, he didn't exactly get off to an inspiring start. When asked by a reporter why he was the best man for the job, Kim replied: 'I have taken the Labor Party from behind before.' Well, no wonder they're so rooted. However, on the upside, at the press conference accepting the leadership, he did manage to bang through 34 questions in 18 minutes. (Or approximately the same number of questions Eddie McGuire gets through in a whole year of *Who Wants to Be a Millionaire?*)

Mr Beazley also claimed that he was going to give John Howard a scare. Other than revealing that Don Bradman actually voted Labor, I'm not sure how he plans to do this. He went on to say he had a 'new fire in his belly' which was encouraging. (Although maybe he should stop eating spicy foods and take some Mylanta.)

For me Beazley's major problem is he can't seem to grab an issue by the balls. Some of his responses are so long and complicated, you wonder when they are going to come out in book form.

Here's a simple guide, Kim: Try and answer a question before Sam and Frodo find the ring. Come to think of it, it's actually pretty amazing that he has a weight problem because he barely pauses long enough to eat.

Everyone seems to agree on one thing: Things aren't looking

particularly rosy for the ALP. Some pundits have suggested that the next ALP prime minister may not even be a member of parliament yet. I think they're being too kind; the next PM is yet to be conceived.

Personally, I'd love to see a female leader of one of the major parties, but I admit there are question marks all over Julia Gillard. After all, she did support Mark Latham, which is like saying you gave relationship advice to Wayne Carey, or media management to Damir Dokic.

Then there's the voice, which I quite like, but even Shannon Noll might think: 'Wow, you're a bit nasal!' When she is attacking the government in parliament she sometimes sounds like a Dalek. 'The government must be overthrown . . . exterminate . . . exterminate!'

But it seems her major stumbling block is that she's of the Left. To claim the leadership, she has to master what Melbourne drivers do every day: the right-hand turn from the left-hand lane.

Then there's Kevin Rudd, your old-fashioned politician who knows that the true essence of politics is keeping the government honest. That, and getting your head on *Lateline* as often as possible.

The problem with Kevin Rudd, or Heavy Kevvie, Pixie and Knucklehead (apart from having more nicknames than Puff Daddy) is that even Harry Potter might look at him and say, 'Wow, you're a dork!'

I'd call him an egg-head, but that would be unfair to Humpty Dumpty. Kevin Rudd is so much of a nerd that at high school he flushed his own head down the toilet.

But should this really be a problem? After all, it's not as if John Howard is the reincarnation of The Fonz. In fact, the ALP could turn it into a positive: 'Vote Labor. We have our own nerd too!'

Ruminating on all this is making me a little bit nostalgic for Mark Latham. Sure, these days you wouldn't touch him with a barge-pole but when he stormed on the scene a few years back, you've got to admit, he had the look of a winner about him. For all his faults, at least he was honest, and he did have energy.

Oh, I can hear you muttering about boisterous buck's parties and bashed-up taxi drivers. But I actually think the Australian public gave Latham an unnecessarily hard time about his private life. Seriously, people, why did we care what Mark Latham did on his pre-wedding night? Unless it involved Paris Hilton, how was it interesting?

Anyway, what exactly constitutes 'behaving inappropriately' at a buck's party? Perhaps there's footage of him sober, with not a stripper in sight, no handcuffs, or any of his mates trying to shave off his eyebrows. Un-Australian!

While we're on the topic, why did we give a flying faction about Latham's so-called 'active sex life' before he was married? If he screwed a few of us when he was single, he mightn't have felt the need to do so again as prime minister.

Instead of making excuses, Mark should have embraced his sex appeal and tried to attract the swinging voters who really like to swing. During the election campaign instead of kissing babies, he should've kissed babes.

But it was Latham's violent tendencies that were said to have damaged him the most. But even then, did people really not vote for him because he once clocked a cabbie? Hasn't everyone wanted to show a taxi driver the most direct route between your fist and their face? That's the reason for those little plastic bubbles. Come to think of it, he should've turned it into an electoral promise and pledged to take a swing at a bank manager, someone from Telstra and Shannon Noll. Not only would he have won the election, he might have been elected Pope.

Look, it's obvious to everyone that Mr Latham has a temper, but he did try his best to hide it. Every time the government threw some mud at him, it was like a scene from *The Incredible Hulk*. 'You're making me angry, you're not going to like me when I'm angry!'

But would it have been such a bad thing to have a PM with a bit of aggro? I'm sure our sugar farmers would've got a much better deal in the Free Trade Agreement if the US were frightened of Latham's Fists of Opportunity.

In his defence, Mr Latham did repeatedly deny that he was a bully and threatened anyone who called him so that he'd flush their head down the toilet.

I did wonder why the muck-rakers in the Liberal Party didn't dig even deeper into Latham's sordid past during the last election. I heard that forty years ago, the former ALP leader used to get in fights all the time, would throw food at people, pull their hair, even hold them down and spit in their mouth. And even worse, apparently he was a bed-wetter. Just as well he never became our prime minister.

Ultimately, though, it wasn't the buck's parties or the accusations of thuggery that lost him the election; it was his own pathetic performance during the campaign. Turned out, Latham's Ladder of Opportunity was actually upside down the whole time. During the campaign, he did so many backflips, the women's gymnastics team were thinking of recruiting him (although they were a bit worried about the size of his boobs).

If you remember, the first thing to go was the ALP's old growth forest policy which was originally designed to protect endangered species in Tasmania. However, it soon became clear that it was actually designed to protect a much more endangered species: the federal Labor MP. But as we all now know, the old growth in the Lodge came up trumps in the end.

But getting back to now. What does Labor have to do to win the next election?

In my opinion, they have to concentrate on reclaiming their heartland. The ALP has lost much of its traditional support from people like plumbers and builders. If Beazley is ever going to be PM, these are the vital votes he needs to win back. Next time he does a press conference, I propose he do it with a bit of arse-crack hanging out the back of his pants.

Beazley has said his aim is to embrace the ordinary voters, but I'm sceptical about this tactic. Who is he getting his advice from, Ross Cameron? I reckon the ordinary voters will be happy with a new tax package, rather than feeling it against their leg.

Some pundits say that if the ALP is to win government, the party must appeal to 'Kath and Kim' land. (But wouldn't Beazley's time be better spent appealing to real people rather than fictional characters? I doubt the next election is going to be decided by preferences from the Lips in *The Mulligrubs*.)

But hey, I guess it's worth a shot. So next election, instead of political jargon like 'Ease the Squeeze' and 'Ladder of Opportunity', Beazley should fix Howard in the eye and say, 'Look at moi, Johnny, look at moi!'. Or how about, 'New Labor, it's noice, it's different, it's unusual.'

Another key demographic the ALP need to reclaim is the youth vote. And that's why I propose they forget about Peter Garrett and draft Casey from *Australian Idol* to the front bench. Not only is she a proven vote winner, but at 55 cents per vote, they can use the revenue to fund most of their policies.

(Plus at *Australian Idol* they let you vote as many times as you like, which is really reconnecting with traditional Labor ideals.)

Some critics have even suggested that the Labor Party should change its name if it is to appeal to aspirational voters. Rather than 'New Labor', why not go the whole hog and change it to something like, 'I can't believe it's not Liberal!'

Or try the opposite and harness people's frustration with party politics by naming themselves, 'Screw the lot of them, they all suck!' I can guarantee if that were an option, the ALP would win in a landslide.

Because the truth is, most Australians are really cynical about the politicians who run (or aspire to run) this country. Let's face it, the majority of both front benches are still largely made up of white men who look like rejects from *Revenge of the Nerds: The Musical*.

We never see anyone in parliament who has actually lived a little. Take drugs, for example. Now I'm not suggesting that John Howard replace Abbott and Costello with Keith Richards and Robert Downey Jnr, but with so many young people experimenting with recreational drugs these days, wouldn't it be good to have a few people in parliament with some personal experience in this area?

At least Mark Latham admitted that he'd tried a little bit of pot – which may explain the man-boobs and some of his weirder ideas: 'Dude, have a toke on that smoke and then ease the squeeze, hey that's a good one, now pass me the Tim Tams of opportunity.'

But when Tony Abbott was asked the same question, he replied that he'd tried pot but didn't inhale. Who rolled the joint, Tony, Bill Clinton? Let's hope you didn't share any other habits with Big Bill or one day you might be confronted by a cigar that claims you're its father.

But all jokes aside, it's this sort of political double-speak that really alienates the younger voters. After all, are young people going to trust someone to manage the economy when they can't even work out how to smoke a joint?

Why would you smoke and not inhale? You're still breaking the law, but not getting any fun. It's like drinking, and then spitting it out, or having sex but not wanting to orgasm. No wonder most kids would rather listen to Cypress Hill than Capital Hill.

I'm not in any way suggesting that MPs should lounge around smoking pot – although it would give a whole new meaning to the term 'joint sitting'. Not much would get done if John Howard threw over his duties as Member for Bennelong and instead became the Member for Have-a-Bong. And I'm not sure the parliamentary canteen is equipped to handle Kim Beazley, Joe Hockey and Amanda Vanstone with the munchies.

All I'm saying is young people might feel more connected to the political system if they could relate to some of the people who are representing us in parliament. Our society has such a narrow definition of what makes a good leader, and the main prerequisites seem to be based on American sit-coms: white, male, married with kids.

Julia Gillard is a good test case. Everyone reckons she can't be leader of the ALP because she's a single woman without any kids. So what? While experience at managing little brats may be helpful in running the ALP, in this day and age do we really care if she is childless?

Is Sharelle who has ten kids to eleven different fathers and works the 8–items-or-less aisle at the local supermarket ten times more qualified to lead the country than Julia Gillard?

'What would she do at official functions?' the letter-writers asked? Hmmm, I'm guessing she would probably go by herself. Come on, people, it's not as if she is going to cause an international incident by taking a vibrator as a date. 'Mr President, this is my significant other, Mr Buzzy.'

Who cares if politicians have 'interesting' sex lives anyway? I don't really want to think about John Howard having sex. 'Oh gee . . . touch my tax package . . . come on, it's 10 per cent bigger . . . I want to do to you what I've done to the country . . . I love you, George, oops I mean Janette.'

But just to get serious for a minute, aside from being humourless, anachronistic and uninspiring, today's politicians don't seem to have a clue when it comes to policy. Consider Brendan Nelson's introduction of Voluntary Student Unionism as an example. Justifying this latest act of butchery on our education system, Nelson argued that students shouldn't have to pay for something they do not use. Cool. Well, in that case, I'm not paying for my degree. Thanks, Minister.

Wouldn't it be great if the world operated by Brendan Nelson's rules and we never had to pay for anything we didn't use? I'd get a nice refund for those rollerblades that are still in the box at the bottom of my cupboard.

It would certainly throw the whole tax system into disarray. For starters, can I have my baby bonus money back? The only baby in my life is Baby John Burgess, so why should I pay for every Sally who was dicked by Tom to pop out a poo-and-spew machine?

In fact, give me a refund on all my taxes that go to kids. I don't have any so why should my money go towards vaccinating, feeding and educating them? (And while we're at it, can we legislate to store all crying babies on planes in the overhead lockers?)

Sure, in the past I didn't mind my taxes going to childcare because I assumed it was part of living in a society. But the Libs are right: in today's world, it's user pays.

So while you've got the chequebook out, Mr Costello, can I have some of my Australian Film Commission money back please? You see, I don't watch Australian films – it takes too long to get rid of the stink afterwards – so a refund would be appreciated.

And where do I apply to get my money back for those Medicare ads? They were so bad, Ben Affleck would've been perfect for the leading role. My Jewish friends were forbidden to watch them because they were too hammy.

Also, I wasn't really that keen on the war in Iraq. In lieu of cash, I'd be satisfied with some night-vision goggles or a tank to help me negotiate my way through peak hour.

I did love the recent Commonwealth Games, so I don't mind my money going to the Australian Institute of Sport but I didn't watch any of the synchronised swimming – in fact, I don't even consider it a sport – so you'd better refund me that money too.

But getting back to VSU: You see, some would argue that the student union is about more than cheap sausage rolls and left-wing rabble rousers. In fact, the union sponsors a lot of on-campus entertainment. Without that budget, campus life will only be exciting on the rare occasion that the Newcastle Knights play a game in town.

And I understand some people resent paying for things they don't use – like childcare or counselling. (Although if a few more parents left their kids in a crèche instead of at the Neverland Ranch, the world would be a much better place.)

The point is, it's good to know these services are available. Who knows, you might need them one day. (If the student union can no longer afford to hand out free condoms, more and more students might be starting their BA but leaving with a BA-BY.)

The concept of user-pays is all very well, but think about it in practical terms. Will the pot-head who needs drug rehabilitation be able to afford a counsellor, particularly after he's blown his money on Tim Tams? The user won't pay.

Instead of complaining about the union fees, why don't students take advantage of services offered? You've paid, so use. Look at it this way, at most uni bars the beer is at least 20 cents cheaper than everywhere else. So that means if you drink five beers you've already saved a dollar. All you have to do is drink ten beers a night for the first 150 days of uni, and for the rest of the year, every drink you have is pure profit. Now that's an equation even Peter Costello might appreciate.

So, is it any surprise most young people have no faith in the political system? Let's face it, most of them would rather vote for Shane Warne, because at least with him you know at some stage he's going to try and screw you.

(Although there is no truth he has dubbed 'Little Shane' the 'Minister for Foreign Affairs'.)

When it comes to sticking it up the youth, this government puts Mick Jagger to shame, and they had the pants around their ankles again recently when they moved to close voting enrolment almost as soon as an election is called.

It begs the question, why would the government want to make it harder for people to get involved in the electoral process?

It's like John Howard has turned into a James Bond villain. Next he'll be stroking a cat and cackling: 'Yes, you can vote, but only after you complete this series of tasks, each more complicated than the last.'

Of course the changes to voting regulations will affect everyone, but the group most likely to suffer are first-time voters. Obviously, the government is like my grandpa, it believes young people should be seen, and not heard. (Then sent to war to be shot and not heard.)

Look, I'm not saying young folk can't make mistakes when they vote. After all Shannon Noll only came second in Australian Idol, and he is clearly the greatest talent this country has ever produced. And very handsome. And that hair on his face looks really cool, honestly. (Please don't hit me.)

Think about it, the next generation may not be interested in politics, but thanks to reality TV they have certainly been raised on voting. They're probably just confused about why they have to go to a primary school on a Saturday to do it, instead of just texting 'John Howard' to 199EVICT.

For those who haven't been following the story, the other amendment the government made was to make it illegal for prisoners to vote. Well, that'll teach them a lesson, won't it?

I'm sure now that this rule is in force, incarceration rates will be slashed. People who, before this, were so desperate they were willing to risk sharing a jail cell with a bloke who wants to play 'Keith and Nicole's Honeymoon' and will be turned away from a life of crime.

Even criminal masterminds will be thinking: 'Well, I was going to rob that bank on the weekend, but local council elections are coming up. Do I really want to risk my chance to express my opinion on what day bin-night should be?'

But I guess maybe the pollies are right, our prisons are filled with liars and cheats who want nothing more than to rip off the general public for their own personal gain. They shouldn't be voting, they should be running for parliament.

However I do think the move to ban prisoners contains some weird logic. Think about it, what normally happens if you don't vote? They send you a fine, and if you don't pay the fine they send you to jail . . . where you're not allowed to vote.

I guess the problem is if people in jail can vote, then political parties might start to target them with policies: 'This election we promise to bring down crime numbers, by not arresting anyone! Plus we promise all jail cells will be fitted with sliding doors, we will be standardising all security codes to 1234, and guard dogs will be replaced by guard kittens.'

But whether it is young people or prisoners, I just don't get the move to exclude people from the political process. Surely in a healthy democracy, we want as many people voting as possible?

That's why, instead of fining people for not voting, I think they should combine the election with Tattslotto.

If you number your Senate ticket in the exact same order as they finish in the election you win a prize, and as a bonus there is a scratchie down the bottom of the form and if you get three Peter Costellos you get a free tax refund.

There is a weird flaw in our system, though. If you are enrolled to vote and don't, you get a fine, but if you don't enrol nobody seems to care.

That's like being pulled over for a speeding ticket, and the cops letting you off when you reassure the officer that you are driving an unregistered car, and you don't have your licence.

Personally, even if voting was not compulsory I think there are three reasons why everyone should vote. First, people die for the right to vote in other countries, so we shouldn't take it for granted. Second, it's your right to bitch about the result. And third it's just an excuse to hang out at a primary school without the restraining order.

People argue in a democracy it shouldn't be compulsory to vote. It's not. It's compulsory to rock up and get your name ticked off the role. Once you are in the tiny cardboard booth you can do whatever the hell you want.

You can 'donkey vote' or as it was known in the last election, 'voting for Mark Latham'; you can rate all the pollies in order from hot to not or you can turn the House of Reps form into a pirate hat, and the Senate into an origami swan.

If you really want to make a protest, you can drop your pants and use the forms as toilet paper. Although I should warn you, technically that still counts as a vote for the Liberals.

Now that prisoners are barred (geddit?) from voting, who'll be next to lose the vote? Perhaps it will be the current public enemy number one. No, not the turkey-slappers. Fat kids.

I was a fat kid when I was at primary school, and I mean really fat. Put it this way, if Tony Squires had been doing a television show on the ABC back then it would have been called *The Wil*.

When I ran, I sweated gravy, when I bent over, the other kids painted Goodyear on my butt, and when I stepped on the scales, it asked me to enter my initials as the new high score.

Sure, plenty of kids that age have puppy fat, but I looked like I had been eating entire puppies, deep-fried in batter.

I was so fat that if I'd gone to the same school as Fatty Vautin, he would have been known as A-Little-Bit-Tubby-But-Nothing-Compared-To-That-Boombah-Wil Vautin.

Yep, kids can be cruel and I heard them all: how they heard a beeping sound whenever I backed into a room; how the Great Wall of China and my arse were the only things visible from space; how I had to wear Levi 5001s; how if I went to war, I'd take my partner Skinny; or even how if I got a bad fake tan, I could go to work for Willy Wonka in his chocolate factory.

It was terribly tough being a tubby tot, so that's why I'm glad our politicians have finally bitten the chocolate-coated licorice bullet and decided to do something about childhood obesity.

With more than a quarter of Australian children now classified as overweight, it's time to admit the Lucky Country has become the Tubby Country.

Former opposition leader, Mark Latham, fired the first shot by suggesting if we banned junk food advertising during kids' TV, Fat Cat, Dorothy the Dinosaur, Big Ted and The Fat Controller could all lose a couple of kilos, and maybe Humphrey could even fit back into his pants.

Personally, I think this is a brave idea. Sure, commercial TV needs ads – let's face it, without ads the last series of *The Block* would have been over in fifteen minutes – but when the only oranges our chubby kids are eating at quarter-time of sports have the words 'Terry's' and 'Chocolate' on them, you know it's time for drastic measures.

Prime Minister Howard responded by saying he didn't want Australia to be a 'nanny state'. Well, unless it is to do with the morning-after pill, drugs, censorship or lesbian mummies (in which case get him a job in a bridal shop in Flushing Queens), let him pash off Mr Sheffield and we'll call him The Nanny.

Mr Howard said under new government plans, kids would be required to do two hours of compulsory physical education a week. This is a good plan, but I don't think it goes far enough. I think they should make Michael Jackson the PE teacher. Now, that would really get the kiddies running.

Then, just when it seemed like we were all getting somewhere, the Minister For Missing-The-Point, Tony Abbott, made the debate personal by sticking the boot into Mr Latham's weight calling him Dr Man-boobs.

Coming from a government who have had to get the front bench reinforced to support some of their boombaladas, this seemed like a case of the pot calling the kettle fat.

Some of Abbott's colleagues aren't just an MP they're an entire electorate, and the only thing they should be shouting out in parliament is 'Bring me Han Solo!'

One minister in particular (whose name sounds a lot like a sport he doesn't seem to play much of) looks like he is smuggling so much crack in his pants I'm surprised Whitney Houston isn't trying to smoke his arse.

That said, if any politician wants to lecture kids about losing weight then they should set an example themselves.

Maybe the weight-conscious politicians should take a leaf out of the Prime Minister's book and start power-walking. You can say what you like about Mr Howard, but he certainly keeps himself fit, although can someone please tell the PM that just dressing in a Socceroos tracksuit does not make you look athletic. At 67 dressed in his trackies he looks less like he should be going to parliament house, and more like he is popping down the Rooty Hill RSL to put a couple of bucks in the pokies.

The most disturbing image of the PM wearing his tracksuit came during the FIFA World Cup when he was photographed in the press watching the Socceroos play, dressed in his green and gold tracksuit, which begs the question, when he's watching the cricket does he get dressed up in white, pads and a helmet?

And please, newspaper editors, no pictures of him watching Thorpie at the Olympics.

NINE

THINGS THAT MAKE ME GO DUMB

One thing guaranteed to give me road rage is 'Baby on board' bumper-stickers. Who cares if there's a bloody baby on board? It's not like I'll spot that stupid sticker and think: 'Well, I was going to run that car off the road but now that I know there is a baby on board . . .'

Seriously folks, unless the baby on board answers to the name of Spice or John Burgess, do us all a favour and keep it to yourself.

Other motorists don't feel the need to point out who is 'on board'. You never see a sticker saying, 'Annoying old tool in hat going 80 in the right-hand lane on board' – although admittedly, it's easy to identify these drivers because the back of their car says 'Volvo'.

Okay, I admit a two-dollar sticker might seem a minor thing to get so fired up about, but lately I've noticed a direct correlation between the type of bumper-sticker on a car, and the quality of driver behind the wheel.

Leading the charge is the 'Honk if you're a hoon' brigade – groups of boofhead blokes in their hotted-up cars, who are not only sharing a ride but also a brain.

You can usually identify these idiots by the 'No fear' emblem on their back windscreen, which should more accurately read: 'No idea what the road rules are'; 'No way any of the girls I yell at out the window will ever sleep with me'; or 'No fear that my penis is anywhere near as big as the muffler on this car.'

These guys are closely followed by what I term the 'Shoot, root and drive a ute' mob who have plastered their 4WDs with slogans like, 'I hunt and I vote' or 'Guns don't kill people'.

I've never understood the purpose of these stickers in Australia. In the US they're a lobbyist tool for special interest groups, but here voting is compulsory. Everybody votes. You may as well have a bumper-sticker that says, 'I poo and I vote' or 'I read Dr Seuss and I vote, on a boat, with a goat!'

And yes, I guess you are technically correct Darren, Sharon (and your kids, Karen and Aaron) when you claim guns don't kill people. They don't, bullets do. But guns help.

Bullets aren't much good if you just chuck them at someone. You rarely hear a report from a schoolyard in the US that says, 'The carnage was terrible, the suspect had a handful of bullets – and a tennis racquet!'

Next up, proving the Highway to Heaven will be gridlocked

come peak hour at the Apocalypse, are Christian drivers.

Now before Matthew, Mark, Luke and John start firing off their complaint letters, I should point out I have nothing but respect for God-botherers, and Christian bumper-stickers are some of the wittiest on the road:

'I considered atheism but there weren't enough holidays'; 'Answer my prayer, steal this car'; 'God is dead – Nietzsche . . . Nietzsche is dead – God'; and my personal fave, 'Jesus had a mullet'.

But just because you know you're going to Heaven doesn't mean you should drive like you have an urgent appointment.

If I get cut off by one more car with 'Jesus loves me' on the back, I'm going to get a sticker printed that says: 'Jesus doesn't love me, he's just using me for sex'.

And I'm certainly praying the Lord has a special parking space in hell for motorists who use their mobile phones while driving. I've heard of people answering God's call, but if you're going to do it in traffic, at least go hands-free.

The Bible-basher who cut me off last week (is there a commandment that says indicating is a sin?) had a bumper-sticker that read, 'God made the earth in 6 days'. I was so mad, when we stopped at the next traffic lights I got out of my car and shouted, 'That's pretty impressive, but *Backyard Blitz* would have done it in 48 hours and they would have sent Adam and Eve to Tahiti for the weekend!'

But without a doubt, the worst drivers in the world are easily identified by their slogan: 'Magic happens'. Yes, magic does happen: you got your licence.

If I get stuck behind one more of these meandering morons I'm going to get out of my car, slice them in half, and say, 'Let's see if magic happens now . . .'

But just when I started to worry that these bumper-sticker bastards were sending me barmy, I discovered I'm not alone in my rage.

I was stuck behind a car that not only had a Jesus fish and a 'Magic happens', but a smarmy sticker that asked, 'What if everybody started telling the truth?'

Underneath it, some wit had scrawled: 'They'd tell you you can't drive, you prick!'

Ah, maybe magic does happen after all.

What would you do if you had the power to make things disappear? No question how I'd use my magic skills: I'd wave my wizard wand and dispose of all spruikers.

Look, I know everyone has to make a living, but if you insist on telling people what's inside your crappy little shop, how about investing in an ad, or at the very least, installing a see-through front window?

And I use the word 'crappy' advisedly, because in my experience, most products that need to be spruiked pull off the amazing combination of not only being ridiculously cheap, but also a complete rip-off.

Is there anything worse than getting looked up and down by a spruiker who then shouts that the perfect complement to your outfit would be a 'lovely nylon tartan hoodie, only six dollars'? (true story).

And what's with the tout having a shout outside the Two Dollar Shop? Surely this is the one business on earth that doesn't need further explanation?

Yet day-in, day-out, it's the same chant: 'We have soap, two dollars; we have soap-on-a-rope, two dollars; we have a novelty soap-Pope-on-a-rope, two dollars; we have genuine Rayban sunglasses, two dollars; we have genuine Chanel perfume, two dollars; we have genuine lumps of dirt, two dollars; we have blank CDs, two dollars; we have the new Daryl Somers album, two dollars; and we have New Zealand five dollar notes . . . just two dollars.'

Yes, okay, we get it. Every freaking thing in your shop is two freaking dollars! I actually figured that out from the name of the freaking shop.

The only excuse for a spruiker out the front of the Two Dollar Shop is if they're having a 10 per cent off sale and everything is $1.80 – and even then, it might be easier to change the name of the shop.

(Sometimes I get so angry at being yelled at outside the Two Dollar Shop, I go inside and spend the next ten minutes asking how much certain items are, just to give them a taste of their own medicine. 'Oh, so this is two dollars. What about this one? Two dollars as well? What a coincidence.')

And why is it that every second spruiker has a cockney accent? Are there any cockneys left in London or are they all out here selling 'Dalai Lama desk lamps at prices you would not Adam and Eve'? All I can say is, where is Ivan Milat when you need him.

Harsh, I know, but outside every second shop in the city there seems to be a geezer shouting rhyming slang through a crappy little PA; it sounds like a live performance of the new album by The Streets.

Half the time, you can't even make out what they're saying. 'These prices are so low you will climb the apple and pears to get on the dog and bone to your mates.' Seriously, you need to employ Alf Stewart from *Home and Away* as your translator.

I'm no Dr Karl (not even Dr Karl from *Neighbours*) but isn't it Newton's fifth law that states, 'The louder you have to yell about a product, the crappier it is'?

Put it this way, you'd never see a spruiker out the front of Tiffany & Co. shouting: 'Come on in, we have diamond rings $100,000; we have diamond and gold earrings $200,000; we have diamond and gold nipple rings $300,000; we have shoes with diamonds on the soles of them $500,000; and if that's out of your price range, why not come in and breathe the air, only $25 a gasp.'

In fairness, spruikers aren't limited to the discount crap emporium. In Melbourne they stand outside restaurants and in Sydney out the front of strip-clubs.

And they use pretty much the same spiel: 'Come in, we have stunning legs, tender thighs and breasts, all covered in a special sauce; and for dessert, bananas, whipped cream and chocolate sauce.'

I'm not trying to shoot the annoying messenger here, and I'm sure life is much harder for spruikers since the invention of the iPod. (Previously you had to walk past the shop with your fingers in your ears going, 'La la la la, I'm not listening' – which is what John Howard did during meetings about the AWB.)

But to combat technology, spruikers seem to have adopted the tactics of an American trying to communicate with a non-English speaker: they just yell louder.

And this is where I reckon the concept of spruiking is seriously flawed. I don't know about you, but if someone shouts at me, I tend to assume I'm not welcome.

Not welcome is how I felt recently when I unwittingly broke the unwritten rules of the 8-items-or-less lane at my local supermarket.

Forget about terrorism magnets, if the government was serious about preventing conflict, they'd send out fridge magnets that explain the proper etiquette for this urban war zone.

In theory it should be simple, but the rules, laws and conventions of the supermarket express lane are so complex, you need Barry Jones to draw you a diagram before you can even begin to understand them.

Let me get all Geoffrey Robertson here and pose a hypothetical. Say I go through the 8-items-or-less lane with three cans of beans – same size, same type – is that one item . . . or three? Most people seem to think it counts as three.

However, your honour, I'm no big-city lawyer, but what if I also buy three apples? Is that counted as three items or just one? The prevailing wisdom dictates that this is only one item because the apples are in a bag. But this leaves me with the question: What happens if I put my three cans of beans in a bag?

Does the bag make all the difference? If so, I could go through that lane like Santa Claus, with a huge sack of groceries. 'Sorry, it's just one item, it's in a bag, stick that up your arse, Lisa McCune.'

And speaking of bags, have you noticed that if you request a plastic bag in a supermarket these days, the response implies you just asked to club a baby seal to death.

Don't get me wrong, I agree that we use way too many plastic bags, but sometimes this environmentalism is taken too far. I can understand not getting a plastic bag for a packet of smokes, but the other day I had three apples, a can of deodorant, two cans of Coke and some toilet paper, and the lovely woman behind the counter asked, 'Would you like a bag?'

Well, no actually, I was planning to juggle this stuff on the way home. Let's swing by hardware and get a chainsaw to make it interesting.

You know what else really bugs me about the 8-items-or-less lane? When you put your groceries on the counter, leaving a respectful distance between your stuff and the person in front of you – and they *still* feel the need to use that little wooden divider. That really pisses me off. 'Hey, man, we should be tearing walls down, not building them.' It's as if they don't want their groceries to touch yours. Why? They all come from the same place, mate. I always feel tempted to pick up the divider and lick it.

And should you be allowed to pay with your ATM card in the express lane? It hardly seems 'express'. Have you ever been stuck behind a pensioner trying to remember their PIN?

You just want to pick up some milk but there they are tapping so many buttons into the machine, you wonder whether they are trying to hack into the Pentagon. Either that, or they've mixed up their PIN and their phone number.

But even worse is the idiot who thinks he is a comedian. Hey dude, earth to tool, no one cares about your lame jokes. Sharelle, Narelle, Chantelle and Janelle are too busy doing a price-check to pretend you're Oscar Wilde. If one more person says, 'Well actually, it's spendings' when the poor girl asks 'cash or savings' then you'd better watch out because I'll shove my 8-items-or-less up your red spot, and when my bag of apples follows, it is not going to be special.

But here's what *really* pisses me off about supermarkets these days. Have you noticed how early they're putting Easter eggs on the shelves? Seriously, if I had a goat, this issue would get it. If I had a can of worms, I would be cracking it open right now.

It's been driving me kooky ever since New Year's Day, when I stumbled into the supermarket with a hangover so big it had its own mushroom cloud, only to be greeted by shiny rows of Easter eggs.

These are the thoughts that raced through my mind: 'Wow, I really had a lot to drink; I've woken up four months later. Crap, I've missed my birthday and more importantly, now I will never know what is down the bloody hatch on *Lost*.'

Even by the standards of supermarkets that seem intent on turning the twelve days of Christmas into the twelve months of Christmas shopping, 1 January seems a tad early. Are petrol prices so high that Santa and the Easter Bunny have to share a ride?

I reckon you've started advertising Easter too early if there is a chance Jesus will come back before you sell all the eggs.

Now let me point out, I'm not having a go at Easter here. Like any man with man-boobs, I love nothing more than commemorating Jesus's death by eating chocolate eggs delivered by a magical bunny (just like it says in the Bible). But do we really need four months of celebration? How difficult can the Easter egg hunt be? Let's be honest, if you told kids that he had a stash of chocolate, Osama would be found in less than four months.

At least with Christmas, people might need time to shop and save, but does this apply for Easter?

I know it might seem like a trivial matter, but I think it reveals much about our society's dependence on instant gratification.

What happened to the joy of waiting? To the anticipation that makes an actual event more rewarding? What happened to 'Don't worry, it happens to all guys, you're probably just nervous'?

I think you see my point. Anyway, if we really want to celebrate Easter earlier, why not bite the bullet and change the date? Instead of 15 April, why not make it 1 April? That's two weeks saved. But isn't that April Fool's Day, I hear you ask. Not anymore. That's now on 26 January.

Sure, that means we had to move Australia Day to 1 January, but now we can do New Year's on 25 December and knock over Christmas on the first Tuesday in November.

Then we can celebrate Melbourne Cup on Halloween, Halloween on 4 July, Independence Day on Anzac Day and Anzac

Day at Easter. Now we've saved a couple of weeks to jam in as many Queen's birthdays as we want!

Seriously though, it's not just the time suction that bugs me, it's the complete commercialisation of Christianity. Now, I've never been known to bash a Bible that wasn't asking for it, but even I find it all a little tacky.

If they're willing to flog Easter eggs for four months, what next? 'Remember, this weekend we solemnly remember the death of the Lord who died on the cross for our sins . . . Speaking of crosses, we have massive discounts in the hardware section all weekend.'

And if the supermarkets are making a buck, it won't be long before the big corporations cash in on it too. 'We all love the story of Jesus feeding the masses with loaves and fish. Here at McDonald's we'll be celebrating this all week with our Fillet o' Fish McMiracle Meal Deal. Would you like absolution with that?'

Or: 'Remember, as the Lord said: Take this pizza, it is my body, and take Coke, it is my blood, and take this garlic bread, it is complimentary! If we don't get it to you by Judgement Day then it's free.'

It's no wonder we have an obesity problem; everywhere you go, someone is trying to flog you massive amounts of junk food.

Take the movies, for instance. The popcorn boxes are so large a family of four could live in them, and the chocolate bars are the size of my arm. 'Are you sure this is a Toblerone? I saw Adam Gilchrist use this to make a hundred against New Zealand.'

Not to mention the drink sizes. Most cinemas don't even offer small anymore. It's either jumbo or extra jumbo or Oh-my-

God-my-drink-is-so-big-Thorpie-is-swimmming-laps-in-it. The piece of ice in my Coke the other day was so big, I reckon it was the one that sank the *Titanic*.

Then there's the combos, which are basically the movie chain's way of saying, 'You know that crap you really didn't want in the first place? Well, for just fifty cents more we can combine it with some other crap you don't really want.'

Still, despite all these so-called special deals, the prices are totally out of control. I wanted to buy a packet of Maltesers the other day, but they cost so much I had to put them on lay-by. It's got to the point where the only person you can take to the movies is your bank manager. You end up spending more than the budget of most Australian films – and you have that same sick feeling in your stomach after.

But while all this is certainly annoying, we must remember that it's not the fault of the pimply-faced kid serving you. All he wants is his eight bucks an hour so he can buy some Clearasil so his forehead no longer spells, 'I've never been laid.' He doesn't really care if you upsize, but he does have to ask. So there's no need to be rude.

I like to make everybody's life a little easier by ordering one size smaller than what I actually want. That way, when the kid asks me if I'd like to upsize, I can say, 'Yes, yes I would. How did you know?'

Speaking of rude, if you are going to spend a couple of hours in a quiet movie theatre with me, please turn your mobile phone off. (And that goes for pagers, beepers, fax machines and pace-makers.) If mobile phones are banned from aeroplanes, why not movie theatres? (And Shane Warne's dressing room.)

If you are so important that you can't have your phone off for an hour or two, then at least set it to vibrate. In fact, receiving a call with my phone on vibrate was the only enjoyment I got out of *Catwoman*.

If it does ring, go outside to answer it. And while we're talking about talking, don't chat during the film or the trailers. If I want someone to talk over the film, I'll watch the director's commentary on DVD.

Don't get me wrong, there are plenty of times when it's fine to have a chat – like during that ad for the movies that shows how much fun you can have at the movies (even though you're already there and no one seems to be having that much fun).

Or in between previews, so you can turn to your mate and say, 'Wow, dude, we have to see that!' or 'Wow, dude, that was the best two minutes and I was still bored' or 'Wow, dude, why do they keep funding Ben Affleck films? Wouldn't it be quicker to flush the money down the toilet?'

But even then, please try to keep it to a whisper. Think of the movies as a church but with better snacks. (And while we're on the topic, please confine your munching to the loud bits of the movie.)

And if you must sneak past me to go to the toilet – that gallon of Fanta wasn't such a good idea after all – a simple 'Excuse me' would be welcome before you wave your bum in my face.

Finally, and most importantly, if you're coming out of a movie with a surprise ending, please remember that there are people in the lobby waiting to see that same movie and don't want to know whether Bruce Willis is really a woman, whether the chick in *The Crying Game* is actually dead, or that Luke Skywalker's dad is really Tony Abbott.

So anyway, you've watched the movie and despite ingesting a silo of popcorn and a jumbo Coke, you're hungry for a feed.

Now, I know I've been pretty vocal about my movie pet hates, but put me in a restaurant and I'm suddenly Mr Meek and Mild.

I wish I could be one of those people who send food back if they don't like it. I just can't do it. Even if it's the wrong meal, I'll eat it rather than make a fuss.

'No, this steak is fine, well actually I'm vegetarian, but I'll just eat the parsley. Oh, and I'm allergic to nuts, sorry can't talk any more, throat closing over. Can I have the rest in a doggy-bag for the trip to hospital?'

Most normal people would send a meal back if they found a hair in it. Well, I could discover Bigfoot giving Guy Sebastian a lap-dance in my mashed potato and I still wouldn't complain.

Even when they ask, 'How was everything?' I still can't tell the truth. No matter how bad the food is, I always hear the same words come out of my mouth: 'Good thanks!' That's why I could never be a restaurant critic; my reviews would always read: 'It was okay; I wasn't really that hungry and I'm sure the vomiting afterwards had nothing to do with the food. Five stars.'

And while we're on the topic of sending back steaks, can I have a whinge about being treated as a second-class citizen just because

I'm vegetarian? It's not so bad in the city, but there are still some places in rural Australia where saying you're a non meat-eater (a member of the mung-bean mafia, the lentilatti, the soy polloi) provokes the worst kind of vitriol.

It's hard to believe but some people are actually *offended* by vegetarians. Yep, they are vege-phobes and they don't want you to come out of the crisper. The argument is always the same: 'Hitler was a vegetarian.' That really pisses me off. Sure, disagree with me for health reasons or just because you like eating meat, but when you say something like that, I begin to suspect that all that mint sauce and gravy has leaked into your brain. (And anyway, the worst dictator of recent times was called the Butcher of Baghdad not Saddam the Salad Muncher.)

But back to restaurants. I have a few recommendations that would make my dining out experience much more pleasurable.

For starters, all restaurants should offer free bread and water. If it's good enough for prison, then it should be good enough for dining out. And please serve the bread with butter as well as olive oil and balsamic vinegar. With the price of petrol these days, I'll put the butter on my bread and feed the oil to my car.

And when did it become so complicated to order a glass of water? 'Would you like tap water, still water, sparkling water, mineral water, iced water, or water wrung specially out of Lleyton Hewitt's headband? Or you could try our house speciality, which tonight is water from the tears cried when Molly died on *A Country Practice*.'

Also, why do most restaurants have fifty types of H-to-the-O, but only one brand of cola? The other night I asked for a Coke, and the waitress said, 'I'm sorry, sir, we don't have Coke.' You don't have Coke? It's only the most popular beverage in the world. Then to add insult to incredulity she added, 'We have Pepsi, it's basically the same, you'll just have to deal with it.' Okay, but I can only pay with New Zealand dollars. They're basically the same, you'll just have to deal with it. (Of course I didn't say that, I just said, 'Okay, thanks.')

And finally, but most importantly, the thing that would really complete my culinary experience is my own, individual pepper grinder on the table. What is it with the pepper-grinder? Seriously, they protect it as though it's some sort of religious artefact; as if it's the actual pepper-grinder that Jesus used at The Last Supper. 'And lo, the Lord did brandish the shaker and with just one twist, manage to season all the meals at the table.'

We are adult enough to use knives and forks, but when it comes to the pepper-grinder, most waiters turn into MC Hammer: 'You can't touch this!' Dudes, chill out, it's just pepper.

I mean honestly, do they think we're going to steal the stuff if they leave the grinder on the table? 'Excuse me sir, is that a grinder down the front of your pants?' 'No, I just really enjoyed the meal . . . Did I mention my name is Matt Shirvington?'

If pepper was really that valuable, you'd see blokes in overcoats out the front of expensive restaurants whispering, 'Psst . . . you wanna score some pepper? It's the good stuff, pure black gold, not cut with salt or anything.'

If any commodity should be treated like gold dust these days, it's petrol. I put a hundred bucks' worth in my car the other day, and that barely got me out of the servo.

It's got so bad that these days, I'll only drive somewhere if I know it's downhill.

If prices go any higher, I'll have to drill a hole in the floor of my car and power it like Fred in the Flintstones. There should be a new show on TV to replace *Millionaire*: Who Wants to Win a Full Tank of Petrol?

With fuel so prohibitive, and airline prices so low, it costs you more to drive to the airport than it does to fly interstate.

If the price of petroleum climbs any higher, rich people will start drinking it at parties: 'Wow, this has a really great texture and body, a strong aroma, and an oily finish . . . 99 certainly was a great year for Castrol.'

Soon, people will think of cars less as a way to get from A to B, and more as novelty containers for storing valuable fuel. That's not just super, dude, it's my superannuation.

Anyway, according to pundits, the problem is the price of crude oil has gone through the roof. (They call it crude oil because when you hear how much it costs, you start swearing like a bloke with Tourette's.)

While all motorists are suffering, some businesses are really copping it. Put it this way, you know there's a problem when your pizza delivery arrives on a horse. (And they have changed their motto to, 'If it isn't there in thirty days it's free!')

These days, if you get into a high-speed car chase with the cops, they double your fine to pay for their petrol.

On the upside, it will have a positive effect on the war on terror. At these prices, no one can afford to make petrol bombs.

But it's not just that oil is seventy bucks a barrel, it's also the tax. Yep, for every litre you put in the car, about fifty cents goes to the government. Which would be fine if all the roads were perfect, but at that rate, not only should there be no potholes, but the white lines should actually be cocaine.

But the pollies don't understand the pain ordinary Australians are feeling. After all, when was the last time they had to pay for petrol?

I'll tell you one thing, though, since petrol started retailing at ten dollars a shot-glass, people are really trying to get their money's worth. Suddenly everyone is like an old man at the urinal trying to shake out those last extra drops.

And while we're on the subject of service stations, what ever happened to the service? Back in the good old days when they practically paid you to take their petrol away from them, they'd come out and fill up for you. But now that you have to take out a second mortgage to drive to work in the morning, you've also got to put in the liquid gold yourself.

I'm sorry, but for $1.45 a litre they should not only fill your car, they should pump up your tyres and wash your windshield as well. In fact, for $1.45 they should do it in a bikini. With their boobs. Okay, I've really got to stop getting all my ideas from Jessica Simpson film-clips.

You're probably getting sick of reading my rants and raves, but indulge me a little longer: I've got to vent about mobile phones.

For one thing, why do they keep coming up with new technology? It seems like every minute they invent a new thing to shove in your phone. Even the most basic model now comes with a camera, stereo, alarm clock and internet. My phone is actually better set up than my apartment. (Though despite buying it this morning, it's already out of date.)

Needless to say, shopping for a new phone is a total nightmare: 'Hmmm, should I get the one with the video camera in case I start dating Paris Hilton, or pay a bit more to get the entire showcase from *The Price is Right*? Or maybe I should get the new Nokia that allows me to travel back in time.'

Personally, I reckon the boffins should spend a little less time trying to cram a microwave and tanning bed into the phone, and more time developing one that gets decent bloody reception. Seriously, my phone is so technologically advanced NASA could use it to launch a rocket, but it still drops out more often than Mark Philippoussis in the first round.

Every time I make a call, I get a brief insight into what it will be like to live in rural Australia after the full sale of Telstra.

But at least I have a lot of great photos to show my friends: 'Look, here's me shouting, "Can you hear me? Can you hear me?"; and here's me saying, "I'll just move around and see if I can get better reception"; and here's one of me standing on the roof with a coathanger in one hand yelling, "Can you hear me now?"; and finally, here's a video of me ringing them back from a landline.'

(Although for all my bitching, I do enjoy having internet access on my phone. I bet I was the only person at the Nine Inch Nails concert who was checking the Western Bulldogs football results.)

Mobile technology's other great advancement is their size. Do you remember how big mobiles used to be? You practically needed a forklift to carry them around. They looked less like phones and more like the gateway to the magical kingdom of Narnia. If you had one in your pants, people kept mistaking you for Matt Shirvington.

These days, phones are so tiny even Barbie's mobile is bigger than mine. (Although I do live in Sydney, so my flat is much smaller than hers.) Instead, now it's the phone's instruction manual that should come with a forklift. Can you remember the last time you bought a mobile, and the instruction book was actually thinner than the phone?

I got a new mobile almost six months ago, and I've just finally finished wading my way through all the instructions, diagrams and warnings. (Although I'm now so intrigued I can't wait for the sequel.)

It seems that the smaller the phone, the larger the book. My mobile is so thin even Kate Moss thinks it should eat more, but the instruction pamphlet reads like a shooting script for *Lord Of The Rings*.

Seriously, it was so enormous I was tempted to ask if anyone had the Cliff Notes. I was searching the store for the Motorola V3 book-on-tape. Although the good news is I can now put a cloth over the book and use it as a fancy coffee table.

My phone on the other hand is tiny. These days it's all about how big your TV is, and how small your phone is, and don't you dare get that the wrong way around.

Yep, it's the only time you'll hear blokes boasting about how tiny theirs is compared to their mates'. If there is a bulge in their pocket it really does mean they are happy to see you.

(My mobile is either really little, or a normal sized phone that has just been in cold water too long.)

My new – or should I say new-ish now – phone is advertised as being only slightly thicker than a credit card, which is not quite as cool as it seems. Especially after the other night when while drunk I tried to stick it into the ATM to get some money for a late-night kebab.

The phone actually came with a warning sticker that said the detachable parts may choke children. (I have been on a few long-distance flights next to screaming brats where I would have considered that a design feature.)

But the truth is detachable parts aren't the issue, my phone is so small most kids could probably get the whole thing in their gob thinking it's a fun-size Kit-Kat.

And because it is so tiny, they have obviously had to sacrifice in some other areas, like battery life.

I mean, yes, it's great my new handset fits neatly into any of my pockets, but this is slightly offset by having to plug my phone in to recharge after every single call.

Sure the phone weighs practically nothing, but having to carry around the backpack with the charger and extension cord is a pain, and towing the mobile generator is really starting to shit me.

But I guess my main problem is that I'm just not good with instructions. I'm at the stage where I think all phones, iPods and computers should come with a ten-year-old kid to show you how to use them. (On the downside if this were the deal Michael Jackson would open his own Harvey Norman.)

I'm hopeless. I opened the first page of the book and it was like everything was written in a foreign language. Then I realised I had it the wrong way around, and it was actually a foreign language.

(On the upside I now know how to ask for the Crazy Frog ring-tone in five different languages.)

But in my defence, there does seem to be a lot of unnecessary detail in the book. For example, there is an entire chapter dedicated to turning the phone on and off.

Get this, to turn it on apparently what you have to do is 'push the on button', and to turn it off you have to 'push the off button' . . . or show it pictures of Shane Warne in Playboy undies.

My phone also has blue-tooth, but I have absolutely no idea how to use it, or to be perfectly honest what it is.

To me blue-tooth sounds like a medical condition you get from not flossing after eating Smurfs or getting your mouthwash mixed up with your toilet cleaner.

I have a theory there is a time in everyone's life where you realise technology has passed you by, and I think my time has come.

I love how in most Hollywood movies you can hack into the most powerful computer in the world in under 30 seconds, but it takes me three days to work out how to program AC/DC's 'Thunderstruck' as my ring-tone.

What's worse is my booklet was obviously designed so that any idiot could understand it, but I still struggled through it like George W. Bush trying to make sense of James Joyce's *Ulysses*.

It actually had a series of diagrams that showed you how to do everything. Kind of like a Mobile-Phones-For-Dummies.

Unfortunately it seems I need a Mobile-Phones-For-Dummies'-Even-Dumber-Dumb-Ass-Friend because as far as I was concerned the pictures in the book seemed to have absolutely no correlation with any of the buttons on the phone.

Me trying to decipher these pics has been like Stevie Wonder playing a game of Guess Who. After six months of staring at the drawings I still have no idea how to send an SMS, a MMS, or a PMS ... although there is a slight chance I may have almost unlocked the mystery of the Da Vinci Code.

Almost, because there's still one thing the manual couldn't explain: why would you buy (and spend half your lifetime learning to use) a sleek, Barbie-accessory-sized mobile if you're going to hide it in your pocket and use those tiny hands-free headsets?

Sure, they're practical for the car, but here's some news for those who insist on wearing them all the time: You don't look cool, you look like you're on your break from the drive-thru window at McDonald's.

And not only do you look ridiculous, with all that talking to yourself, I worry that soon you'll start shouting at me about Jesus.

(Come to think of it, maybe we should pair up tools on their hands-free mobiles with crazy people so that when they walked down the footpath talking to themselves, it would seem like they were having a conversation.)

But all joking aside, I do think our mobile phone addiction is getting out of control. Apparently, kids as young as six now have mobile phones. I'm sorry, but why does a six-year-old need a mobile?

'Hey Cindy, can you cancel my three o'clock wedgie please? I just realised it's the first day of the month so I'm snowed under with pinching and punching. Oh, and can you book me in at the clinic, I think during kiss-chasey I might have contracted girl's germs.'

Speaking of weird baby stuff, did you see that story about the Perth couple who tried to flog the naming rights to their baby on eBay? It must be the first time in history a birth has also been a product launch. All I want to know is, if the product is recalled, do they have to put the baby back?

Clearly, advertising has taken over our lives. These days you can't even watch a movie without being bombarded with product placement. If they re-made *Crocodile Dundee*, Mick would say: 'That's not a knife, this is a knife. A beautiful stainless steel Ginsu stay-sharp, but wait there's more . . .'

But surely our own names should be sacrosanct? Okay, I admit that naming your child after a brand isn't exactly a new idea; these days the schools are full of kids named Mercedes and Lexus. (Funny that no one ever calls their kid Barina or Torana. If you had a really slow kid you could name him Volvo.)

But in my opinion, selling off the naming rights to your baby is completely disgusting. In fact, the only time it's okay to sponsor a child is if they're standing next to Rebecca Gibney.

If you're that keen to exploit your child for cash, why stop there? Why not offer to tattoo the sponsor's name on their skin? Obviously the forehead would be premium space, and the foreskin a short-term investment, especially if the child is Jewish.

Thankfully, companies haven't shown much interest in this perverted proposal. And no wonder, because let's face it, it's a pretty big risk. You've no way of knowing what the kid will be like. Sure, you might luck out and sponsor a future celebrity like Nicole Kidman or Ivan Milat, but the kid might also be like Natasha Ryan and hide in a cupboard for five years. What a waste of cash.

But some marketers claim the idea has merit because it'd be like having a walking billboard – although remember this is a child we're talking about, so more like a crawling, drooling, vomiting, barely coherent billboard. Perfect for companies who normally sponsor rugby league.

As most sponsorship contracts these days contain mandatory good-behaviour clauses, would the company be within its rights to cancel the name if the kid wet his bed, or was spotted picking his nose in public?

The more I think about it, the more I reckon this mad idea is not that far off. After all, these days triumphant sportspeople thank their sponsors before their families and fans. Not so hard to imagine a world where this extends to naming rights of children. Before we know it, we could be welcoming Nicorette Warne, Just Do It Hewitt, or even little Fully-Sick Thorpe.

The way we're heading, classrooms of the future will sound like this:

'Okay, class, settle down. Red Spot, sit down, no one thinks you're special, and Lipton could you please stop jiggling?

'Okay, roll-call, now can anyone tell me why Fleur comes to class three days a month? And if Pizza Hut doesn't get here in thirty minutes . . .

'Mactime, could you please stop licking KFC's fingers. Mactime . . . now!

'Nappy-San, if you challenge me one more time I'll give you some stains you won't be able to remove, and Optus could you please stop answering "yes" to every question I ask? You just haven't been the same since Telstra dropped out.

'Listerine, if you keep up that language I'll have to wash your mouth out. Tally-Ho and Tim Tams, why are you always hanging out with the stoned kids?

'Pepsi, could you please stop provoking Coke, or I'll have to put you by yourself like Solo. And Jack Daniel's, separate yourself from Coke. I know you think you go well together, but it always leads to trouble.

'Kit-Kat, stop giving everyone the big finger or I will have to break you up. Stop listening to M&M and get down the back with Smarties. And Mars, how about a little less rest and play, and a little more work?

'Canon, could you please stop copying, and White Out, restrain yourself from correcting other people's work or I will have to contact your Uncle Toby.

'And VB, I want your assignment. Matter of fact, I want it now! What? It isn't done? Oh, why can't everyone be like Viagra and work hard?'

TEN

DUMBER HOMES AND GARDENS

They say that buying your house is The Great Australian Dream – which I don't really think is true if you are a bloke.

Let's be honest. If you are an Aussie bloke, The Great Australian Dream is probably scoring 100 on debut against the Poms in the Boxing Day Test, and then celebrating in a spa with the Macpherson sisters.

However, despite this, I have been thinking about buying a house. Now before I go on, I should point out, I can't really afford a house. To be perfectly honest, I can barely afford to order the DVD box set of the TV series *House* from Amazon.

But I thought I may as well scan the real estate section of the paper anyway, and after visiting a few places I've come to the conclusion that real estate agents are the only people that John

Howard could look at and say: 'Wow, you're a liar!' Is it just me, or do the descriptions in the ads have absolutely no correlation at all with what the place is really like?

It's as if the real estate agents sit around in an office all day saying: 'This place has a leaking tap, should we fix that?' 'Nah, bugger it, put in the ad it has "water views".' And certainly don't take any notice of the number of bedrooms they list, because in the world of real estate ads any room you could possibly squeeze a bed into seems to count.

'Okay, I guess technically this could be a bedroom, but I think the flushing toilet would wake me up, and the constant dripping of the water views is really annoying.'

Another real estate speak classic is 'charming'. I mean, how can a house be charming? Does it always open the door for you, and present you with a martini when you walk inside?

Same goes for 'generous living room', which makes it sound like every time you go in there the couch will give you a back massage, and the TV will have taped all your favourite shows for you.

'Sparkling floorboards' may sound great, but what it really means is 'we had to rip up the carpet to get the bloodstains out after the series of murders'.

While 'excellent views' means if you happen to be on the roof, on a ladder, you might get a view of the water, more importantly you will get a view of the neighbour's daughter sunbathing.

'Cosmopolitan feel' means someone has left a few *Cosmo* mags next to the toilet out the back. (It may also have a '*Cleo*' feel', a '*Guns and Ammo* feel', and a '*Big Jugs* feel'.)

'Close to shops' means the bloke next door sells stolen goods out of the boot of his car. (And while we're on the topic, I don't think you should be able to advertise it as being a 'stroll to the beach' if you have to change postcodes. Yes, it's a stroll – if you're Jane Saville.)

Same goes for 'spacious interior' which is what most of them would have – if they were a car. I'm sorry, mate, but if this is a 'spacious' house then the previous owner must have been a Mrs White who shared with seven really short blokes.

'Quaint' is basically a nice way of saying 'old and just a tad creepy'. Think the sort of house an old lady might have lived in with her fifty doilies, and sixty cats.

'Sunny' means there is a hole in the roof; 'light-filled living room' means there is a lighthouse next door that will keep you awake all night; and 'modern' seems to mean any place that doesn't have cave paintings on the wall and dinosaurs in the backyard.

And then there's 'cosy'. Put it this way, if you thought the place we called 'spacious' was tiny, then you ain't seen nothin' yet! This place is so small, if you move in the rats will have to move out because there isn't room for both of you.

'Well maintained' is basically code for 'we racked our brains, but we couldn't think of anything else to recommend this property'. Basically it's crap, but on the upside, it's still maintained in its original state of crap.

'Great neighbourhood' means that the place you are going to buy would fall down if a wolf blew on it but all your neighbours have really excellent pads, while 'family neighbourhood' may sound nice but what it really means is there is lots of screaming kids and barking dogs to wake you up early on the weekend.

And don't even get me started on 'perfect for you.' How do they know what is perfect for me? What, does Scarlett Johansson already live there?

But without a doubt, my favourite piece of real estate doublespeak is 'renovator's dream'. Have you ever been set up on a blind date and your friends tell you the person 'has a wonderful personality'?

Yep, basically they call it a 'renovator's dream' because if they called it a 'money pit' a 'relationship ender' or a 'place even squatters wouldn't squat', not a lot of people would answer the ad.

I'm just glad Martin Luther King wasn't a renovator: 'I have a dream . . . of buying a house even Jamie Durie would look at and say piss off!'

Of course, even if you do manage to negotiate your way through the ads, the hard work isn't done. You still have to look through the contract, where they hide the really bad stuff:

'Now, before you sign, have you seen that movie *The Amityville Horror*? No . . . oh well, don't worry then . . . Oh, and did we mention a train runs through your living room every second Tuesday?'

Actually, that's a bad example. If that happened those sneaky bastards would advertise it as being 'close to public transport'.

Let's just imagine that somehow I do manage to find a house that I want to buy. Big call, I know. But you've got to dream. The downside is that I have absolutely no idea how to do it. I mean, maybe it really is as simple as attending a house sale and making the best offer, but then I've been to a lot of garage sales and never come home with a garage.

The first problem is money. The song says 'wherever I lay my hat, that's my home' but I'm here to tell you from personal experience, that won't hold up in court. They call it 'illegal trespass, squatting and criminal nuisance'.

Basically I have examined my finances, i.e. gathered all the loose change I can from down the back of the couch, but it turns out I can't afford to buy anywhere I want to live, and I wouldn't want to live anywhere I can afford to buy.

According to my accountant, I have enough saved to possibly get a time share in a couple of cardboard boxes in New Zealand. Barbie had her Dream House, I would settle for a house with a barbie.

Everyone says when it comes to real estate, buy the worst house on the best street, which is great advice, but I can only afford the worst house in an area where even the people on the worst street would drive through with their windows up.

So not only am I scanning the papers for something I can afford, but if I find something that looks promising, I don't want anyone else to see it and get there before me. I feel like visiting all the newsagents with some scissors and a huge jar of liquid paper.

(Either that, or on open house day just getting all your unemployed mates to stand out the front and pretend to sell people heroin to keep the price down.)

Money is the big issue, and the truth is I just haven't saved nearly enough.

Everything in my flat reminds me of all the cash I have wasted over the years. If only the bank would accept talking Simpsons dolls or The Rock bobble-head as security.

Even my love handles aren't just fat any more, they are a physical embodiment of all the money I have wasted on pies and beer.

So all of a sudden my arse is tighter than Joan Rivers' face. I've found myself saying things like: 'What do you mean you are going to only use that tea bag once? Who do you think you are? Donald Trump?'

Someone asks for a glass of water at the flat and I'm like: 'Well, that will be 50 cents . . . come on, it costs three bucks in the shop, that's still a bargain.'

(I'm even thinking about sending the cats out to get a job.)

So clearly if I am going to make this house thing reality, I need to get someone else to give me the cash.

Of course, there is the first homebuyer's grant, but unfortunately I live in Sydney so instead of giving you the cash they just send a bloke called Grant around to say: 'Mate, there's no way you can afford this place!'

My first impulse was to marry an old rich guy like Anna Nicole Smith did, and then wait around for him to die. But who knew where to begin, so I went to the bank instead.

Wow, it's really hard to get a loan, isn't it? I have to be honest with you, I thought it would be okay, but it's not. Turns out they have all these questions like: 'How are you going to pay it back?'

Hmmm, good point well made. 'I guess I was thinking mainly knob jokes about Warnie and jokes about Amanda Vanstone's weight. If Shannon Noll puts out another crap album, I can probably afford a pool.'

It turns out it's not that easy when you are a comedian to convince a bank you are going to earn enough money in the future to pay back a loan.

You are trying to assure them you will be the next Eric Bana, they think you're more likely to be the next Con the Fruiterer.

The scariest moment of my life was when the bank manager showed me what the house would actually cost if it took me 30 years to pay it off. I'm thinking about taking up smoking, just so I won't have to live that long.

Seriously, there is no doubt in my mind I will die before I ever get to pay it off. I'm not buying a house, I'm buying a coffin I can put a TV and a couch in.

And then there's all the money you have to pay to the government in sales tax. That's tax on money you have already paid tax on. It's ridiculous. At the very least for that sort of coin they should come around and help you pack some boxes.

But the weirdest thing of all is I have found myself looking at places and judging them on what sort of career choices I would have to make to be able to afford it.

'Yes, I know this place is really nice, but is it being shot out of a cannon by Deiter Brummer on *Celebrity Circus 2* nice?'

❖❖❖

They say moving house is second only in trauma to death. Imagine how traumatic it must be to move a dead body. I suddenly have a whole new respect for the dudes from *Weekend At Bernie's*.

I find moving about the most painful thing on earth, with the possible exception of camping, and sitting through the films of Heath Ledger.

If there were a 'Things Wil Hates' Olympics, moving house would certainly get a podium finish.

I hate to relocate, and yet my job means I do it all the time. In the fifteen years since I left home I've moved nearly twenty times. (Although admittedly a couple of those were in the brief period I was in the Witness Relocation Program.)

My dear dad, Graeme, in contrast, has lived in the same house for fifty years – 500 metres down the road from the house he was born in. I've got to say I'm starting to understand the appeal. Even the whole 'marrying your own sister' aspect might be outweighed by the whole 'never having to pack another box full of coat-hangers again'.

Put it this way, you know you really hate moving when you find yourself sitting in the gutter, staring at snails with envy.

Okay, I confess, when you first decide to start packing it isn't that bad. It's even exciting. But that's because the first stuff is easy to pack. All the clothes, books and DVDs fit neatly into the square boxes. (Square stuff into a square box, it's basically kindergarten without the finger-painting and nose-picking.)

But then the degree of difficulty and frustration increases when you discover that no matter how you try and pack it, the same box that will hold fifty books, will somehow only fit six coat-hangers.

And much like trying to pick up at a dodgy nightclub, the longer you are at it, the lower your standards become.

At the start you make sure all the DVDs are in with the DVDs, but by the second day you are putting the recipe books in the same box as your socks, a hammer and the goldfish.

Eventually I find myself caught in the vicious circle of taking all the crap out of the boxes it has been sitting in for the last couple of years untouched, and into new ones where it will sit untouched until I move house again.

Of course, I do also take the opportunity to send as much stuff as I can to charity, and I did throw out some clothes as well. It's kind of sad when you realise you own fashion even homeless people wouldn't wear. (And I did exclude some things on grounds of good taste. I'm not sure a homeless dude would appreciate the irony of wearing a promo T-shirt for *House*.)

Every time I move I am amazed at the amount of crap I have managed to accumulate since the last time. Stuff I can't even remember buying. Like this time I found a DVD copy of Tim Allen's *Jungle 2 Jungle*. I don't think he even has a copy of that himself.

I'm also really bad at doing all the simple things like remembering to redirect the mail. I still have mail being redirected from four addresses ago. Before a letter gets to me, it normally has to backpack halfway around Australia. I just received my Logies invite from 2004.

Choosing the right moving company is really hard, too. I know you should shop around and get an estimate from a moving company before you use them, but to be honest I would prefer they just gave you an estimate of how much of your crap they are going to break.

In the past I have always used the big, reputable moving companies, but as this time I had pretty much spent every dollar I was ever going to earn – and more – buying the house, I just decided to go with the cheapest removalist. You have to start saving sometime.

Which meant we ended up with a couple of wonderful Iraqi guys who had come to Australia as refugees during the war and set up their own business.

As one of them joked, they became removalists after they first removed themselves from Iraq, and I figured that as long as they weren't the guys who moved Saddam Hussein out of his palace and into the hole in the ground, then they were all right by me. Although after the AWB inquiry I have to say I was a little sceptical about the $300 million they wanted to charge me in 'trucking fees'. (And I was pretty suspicious when they said they wouldn't charge me if I let them borrow my passport and driver's licence for a couple of hours.)

But all jokes aside, they were really cool guys and they did a great job. There was one moment – and I'm sure all removalists have to ask this question – where the head Iraqi dude looked at my stuff and said: 'Do any of these boxes contain chemicals?' I couldn't help thinking, oh crap, I've got to ring some sort of hotline. Where the hell is my fridge magnet? Oh, no, they've already packed the fridge.

The next step after buying the house and moving into it, is

throwing the house-warming party, which pretty much means you will spend the next year cleaning up from it.

Seriously, they shouldn't call it a house-warming, they should call it a house-wrecking. There are places in Baghdad that have been bombed that are still in better shape than our new pad. In fact, I think the only reason they call it a house-warming is because at the end of it your place is so trashed the only thing that would make it worse is if you burned the whole thing down.

I just started paying the mortgage, and now it looks like I am going to have to go back to the bank to get a second one just to pay for the damage from the party. The place was in 'great condition' when we bought it, but now it's a 'renovator's dream'.

The house-warming is actually a weird concept if you think about it: 'Hey, we just poured every single cent we had into something we love with all our heart. Do you want to come around, drink all our booze and help us wreck it?'

I mean, it's nice that people bring you gifts, but it would actually be much better if instead they just agreed to replace anything they destroyed at the end of the night.

But part of the reason I wanted to buy the house in the first place was to have my friends around, so you have to be gracious. 'Hey, thanks for coming. Oh no, don't worry about it, I think the carpet actually looks better with the red wine and pizza on it . . . very Pro Hart.'

On the upside, at least you are reminded of how great the party was for the next few months every time you discover yet another hidden stubby lid or cigarette butt.

It's actually amazing all the weird and wonderful places you keep finding crap. You pick up a pot plant, and somehow it seems to have a wine bottle, half a dozen empty beer cans and a cigarette packet underneath. It's like the world's crappiest pass-the-parcel.

I'm starting to think Osama isn't in hiding after all – he probably just went to a cave-warming and someone misplaced him.

If the best thing about having a party is you get to be surrounded by all your friends, the worst thing is you have to be the host. There is always a point when I just give up. Suddenly I get a little drunk and I'm like: 'Come on everybody, let's trash this place . . . oh hang on, this is my place!'

I'm also the guy, when it gets to three in the morning, who says: 'Hey don't worry about going around the corner for some cheap booze, let's just crack open the champagne we got as a house-warming present.'

Yes, I believe wine-tasters will tell you the optimum time to drink a bottle of Moët & Chandon is at three o'clock in the morning when your tastebuds have been completely dulled by a dozen Toohey's and a cask of goon. It really brings out the flavour.

And no decent party would be complete without at least one embarrassing drunken incident. The gold medal goes to a couple of my friends who had not met each other before the party, but soon found themselves very deep in discussion. Very deep.

In fact, they decided the perfect place for this discussion would be the soundproof room off my office (where I do some radio recording) and where they proceeded to discuss each other's brains out.

It all would have been very discreet, and they would have got away with it too, except that the next day I was cleaning up my office, and discovered they had left a perfect outline of their bodies imprinted in the soundproofing on the wall.

We didn't need CSI to discover who the culprits were – we just had to compare bum prints.

We decided to have the house-warming party nice and early so we could get to know the neighbours. And more importantly, to get to know what time they normally call the cops when you have an all-night party.

Turns out they were wonderful and didn't complain at all, which we a) are amazingly grateful for, and b) have taken as an open invitation to have as many parties as we like. (Seriously dudes, you have to set some boundaries.)

Get this, the day we moved in our next-door neighbours even brought us around a freshly baked cake. Seriously, I thought I was in an episode of *Leave It To Beaver*.

The cake was sensational too, the only problem was they brought it around on a really nice plate and we didn't know which house on the street to return it to.

So now I have this picture in my head of everyone in the street bitching about us. 'Have you met the new neighbours?' 'Met them? They stole my plate!' 'Oh yes, the people next door, Mr and Mrs Plate-thief!'

If I knew where they lived, I'd make them something in return, but the one thing my mother never taught me was how to cook. Seriously, it takes me half an hour to make two-minute noodles – and even then I manage to burn the water.

Bugger Aristos, my mates think I'm the real Surprise Chef, because if anything I cook doesn't give them food poisoning, they're really astounded.

When it comes to being bitchin' in the kitchen or great on the hot-plate, you don't have to send away for a fact sheet to know that I'm not your Bachelor of Spatula.

To me macaroni is the dance Peter Costello did with Kerry-Anne; polenta comes out in childbirth; coddling is something you would do with a New Zealander after sux; and as far as I can work out, hummus is some sort of terrorist organisation.

I'm completely culinary-challenged. To me jasmine rice sounds like a drag queen; arrowroot could well be the nickname for archery groupies; kumera is an affordable small car from Holden; and bok choy is the obscure martial art they used in *The Matrix*.

You know the saying, too many cooks spoil the broth? Well, it only takes one Wil to turn a Cup-a-Soup into a Cup-a-Puke.

Put it this way, I lived for two years in a place without getting the gas stove connected; I used the oven as a spare filing cabinet. The flat came equipped with a microwave, which was great for re-enacting the New Year's Eve fireworks. All you need is a metal pot. The only purpose my fridge serves these days is a surface for storing my terrorism magnets.

My idea of a balanced diet is keeping the cupboard well stocked with blue, red and green Pringles, and making sure I drink both local and imported beer. I get my three serves of fruit a day by selecting bananas, raspberries and strawberries-and-creams in my bag of mixed lollies.

But even if I wanted to cook, I wouldn't know where to start. I don't even have a recipe book at home; in fact, the closest I've ever come to food organisation is putting my takeaway menus into alphabetical order.

Not that I can follow recipes anyway. In fact, I think I may have some sort of rare recipe dyslexia. I can't tell a shiitake mushroom from a fuucktake mushroom, and I'd have more luck trying to translate the *Dead Sea Scrolls* than Donna Hay's latest recipe for coffee scrolls.

Yep, I'm the guy who used to think the five spices in five-spice powder were Scary, Sporty, Posh, Ginger and Baby, so is it any wonder I also thought al dente was a character from *The Sopranos* and fusilli was just fustupid that hadn't been cooked properly?

You think I'm joking? I wish. I once tried to cook a Thai curry with coconut milk but gave up when I couldn't find a coconut with nipples. I'm the guy who puts so much salt on his chips, Alissa Camplin tries to ski down them. And you know how I cook cheese on toast? I put the cheese on the bread and then turn the toaster on its side.

Unless you count heating up a few hot chicken rolls at 7-Eleven for my pissed mates, I have never hosted a dinner party. In fact, it's my worst nightmare.

I went to a friend's place for dinner recently and he proudly announced we'd be having an 'Aristos starter, a Jamie main, and a Nigella dessert'. If my mates came for dinner, the best I could offer them would be a 'Ronald starter, a Colonel main, and dessert by Sara Lee'.

But despite my ineptitude in the kitchen, I absolutely love cooking shows. From *The Naked Chef* to Huey, I could watch cooking shows all day. But no matter how much time I spend watching someone else cook, I still have no desire to do it myself. (Then again I also watch a lot of *CSI* and have never felt inspired to cut up a body.)

No, I tend to watch cooking shows in the same way I'd watch porn. Sure, it looks easy and impressive on the screen, but if I tried it in real life, I can guarantee it would be a lot messier.